This Book Belongs to

____

My Friendly Toddler Coloring Book: Fun with Over 200+ Cute Hand-Drawn Illustrations of Letters, Numbers, Shapes, Colors and Animals - Preschool Coloring Book - Early Learner Fundamentals Ages 1-4 by KidzNest Press

Published by Shiny Rocket Publishing LLP
KidzNest Press is a trademark of Shiny Rocket Publishing LLP

ISBN: 978-1-959668-00-8 (print)
Printed in the U.S.A.

First Edition

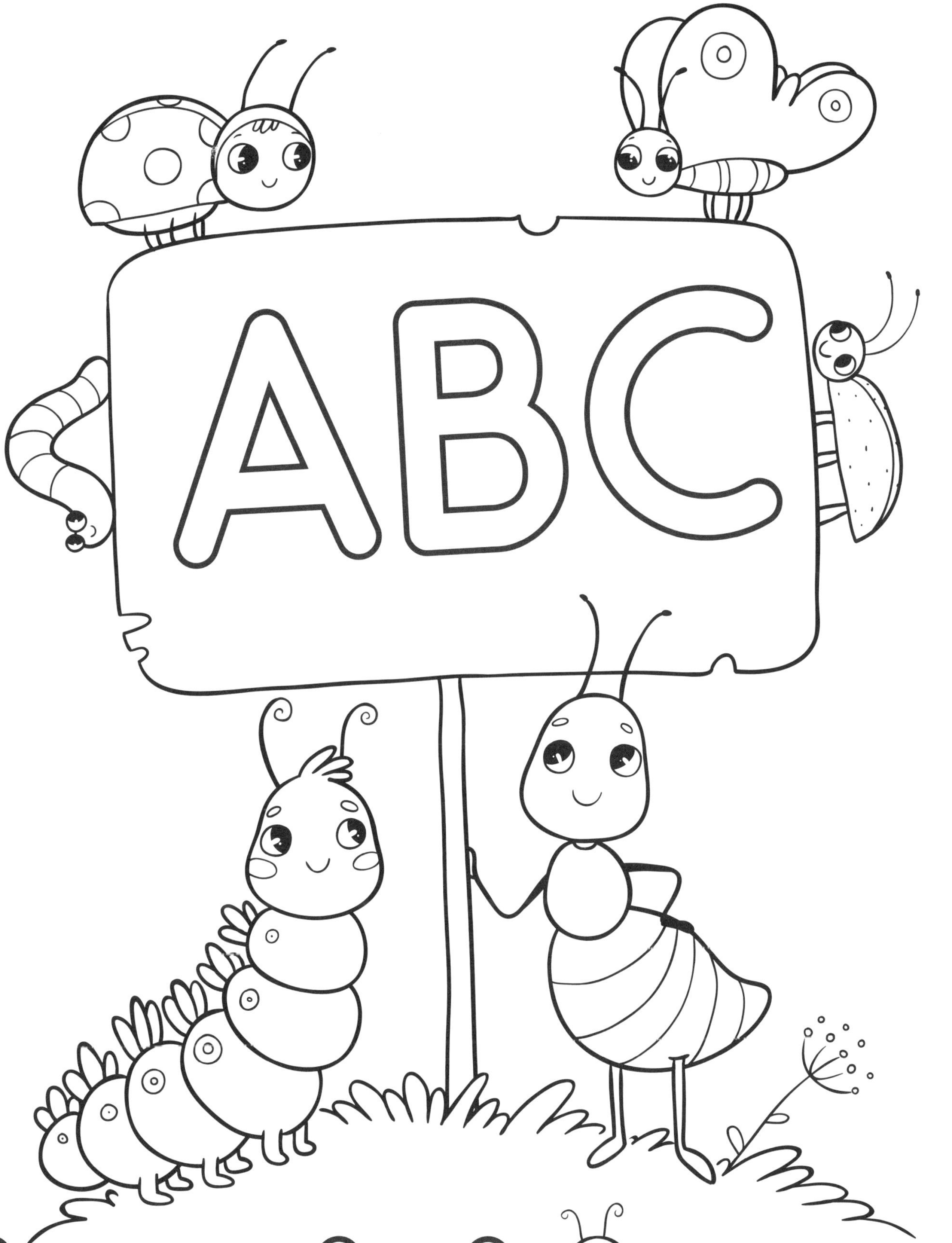

Letters

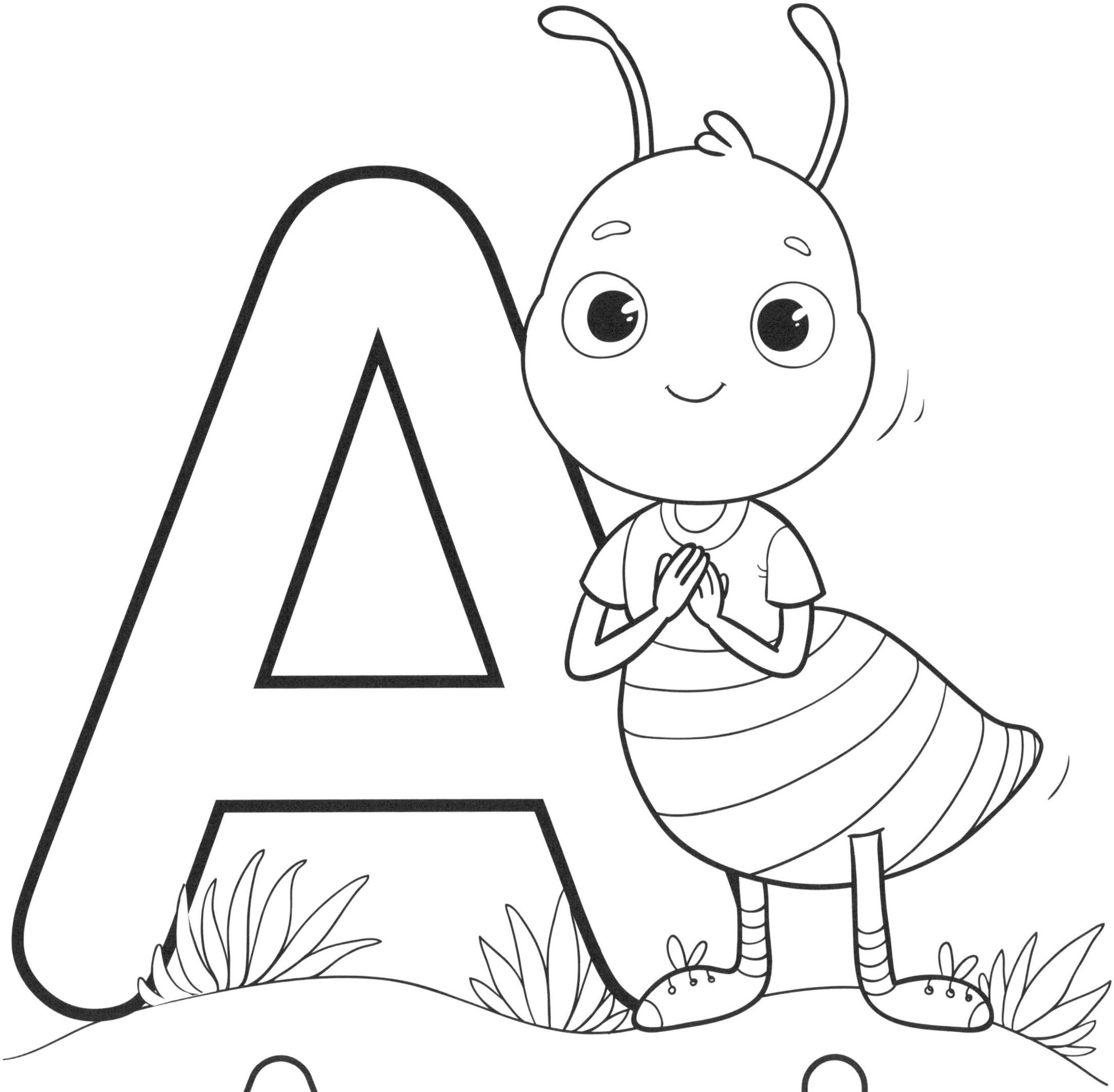

Ant

B

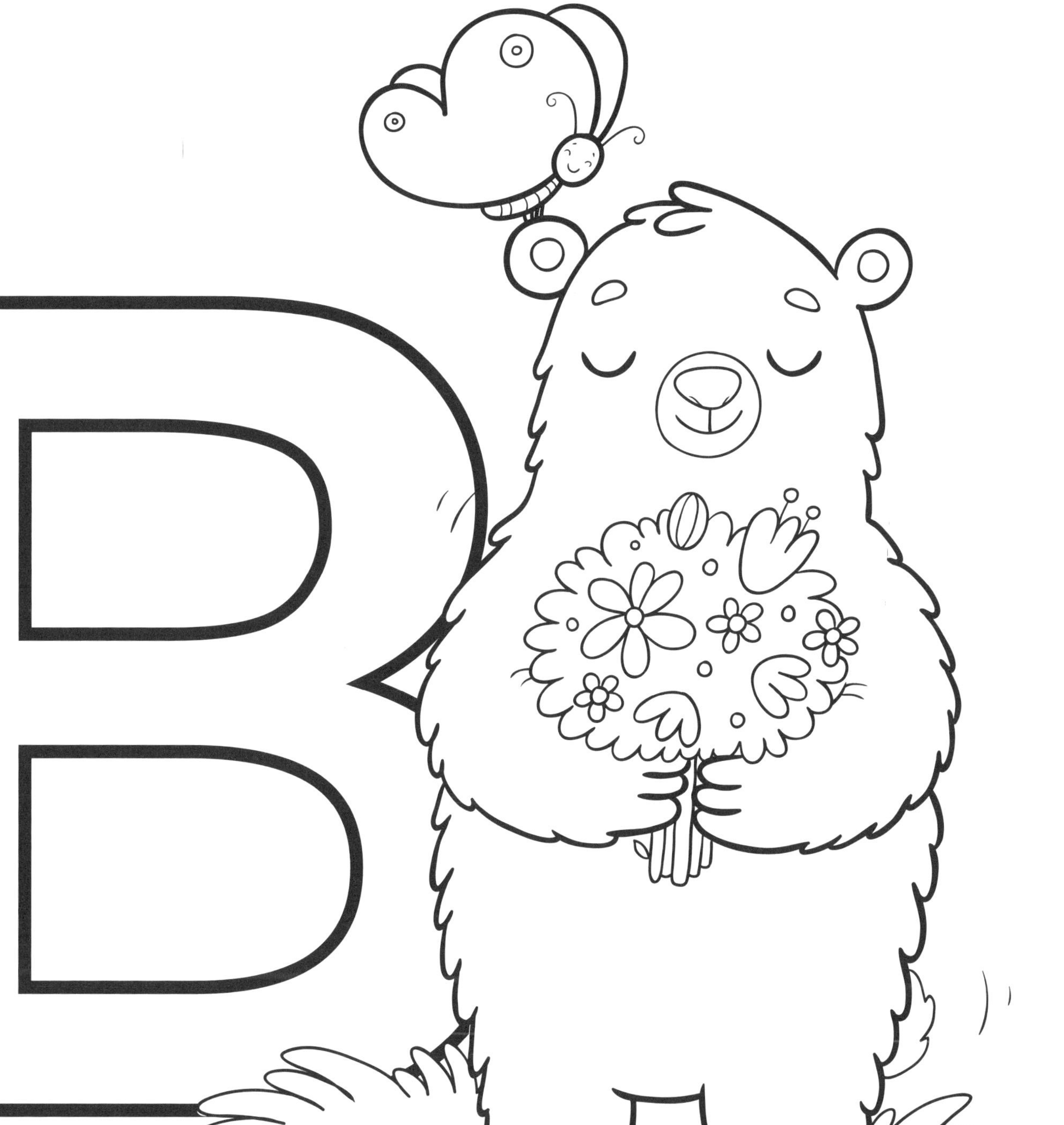

Bear

C

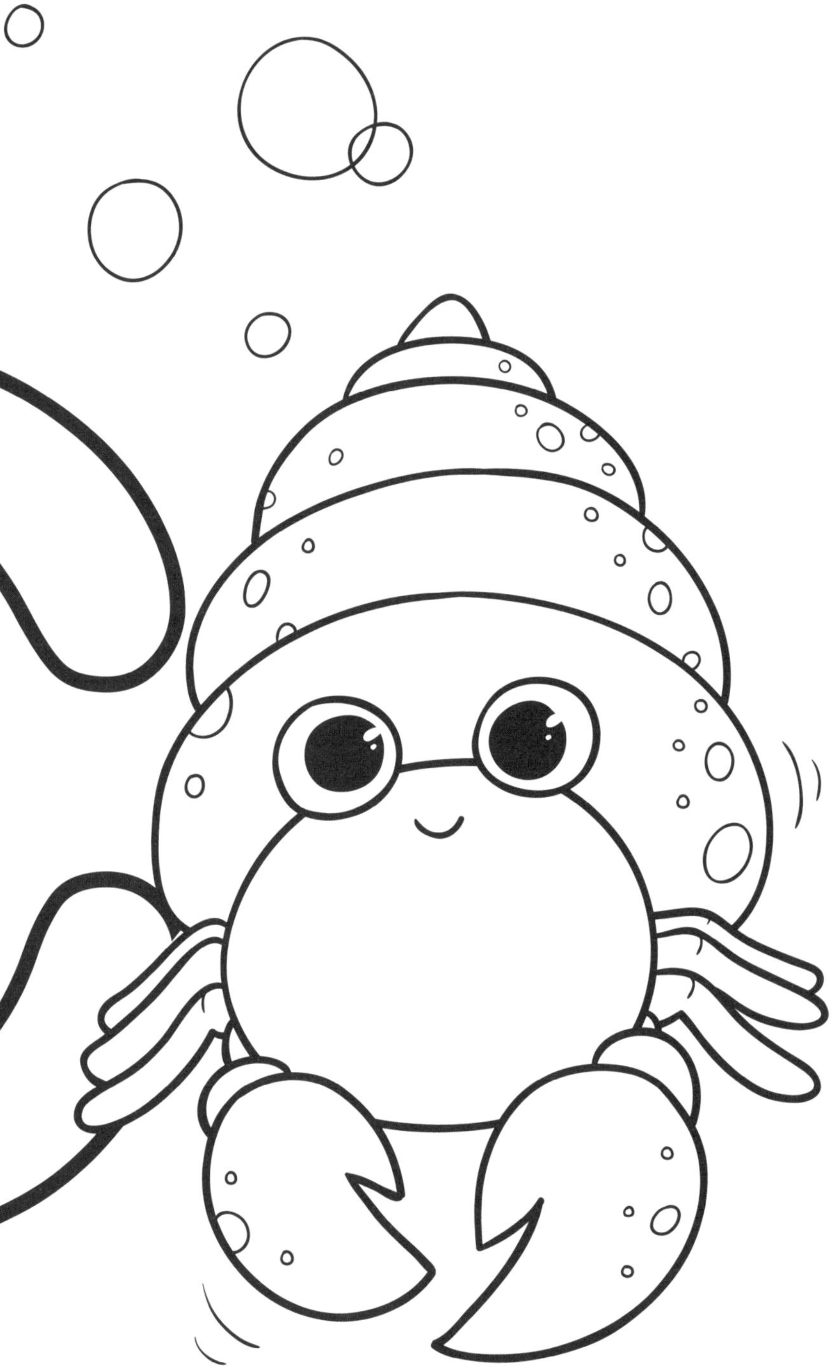

Crab

D

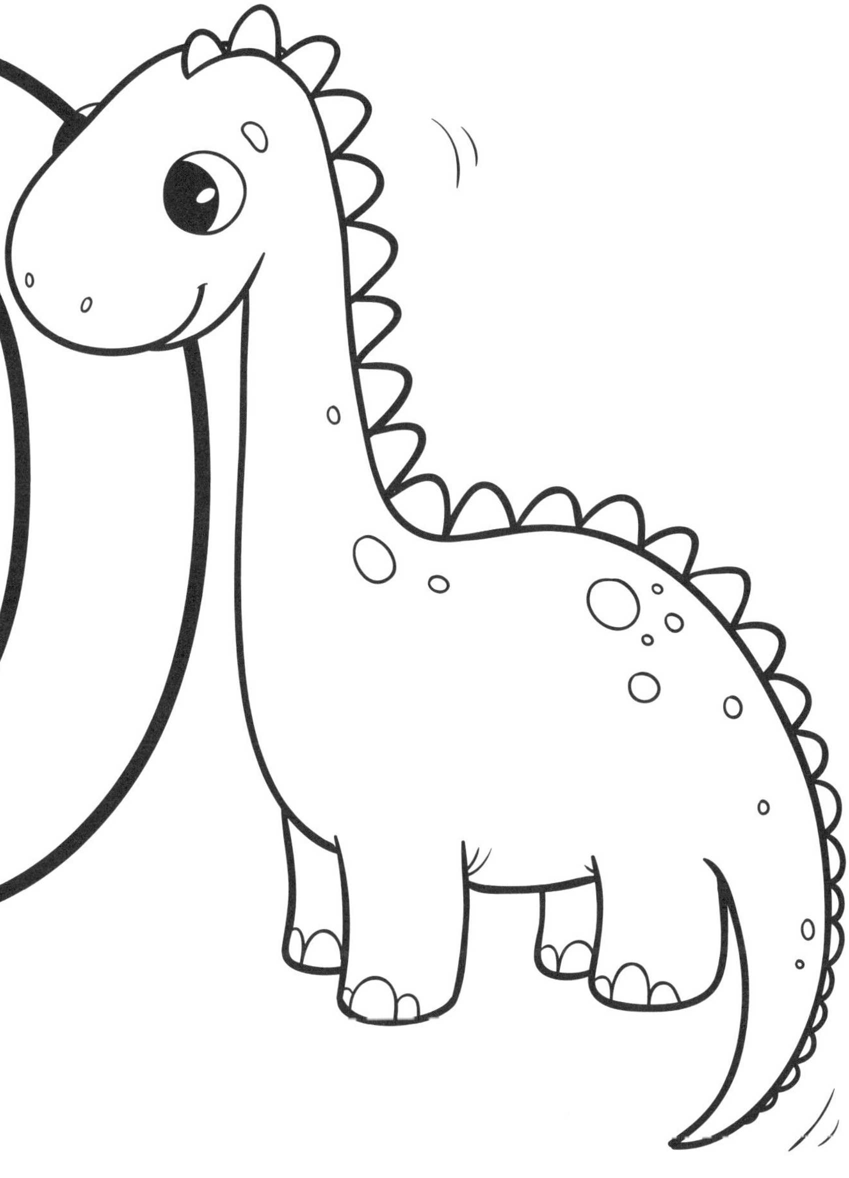

Dinosaur

E

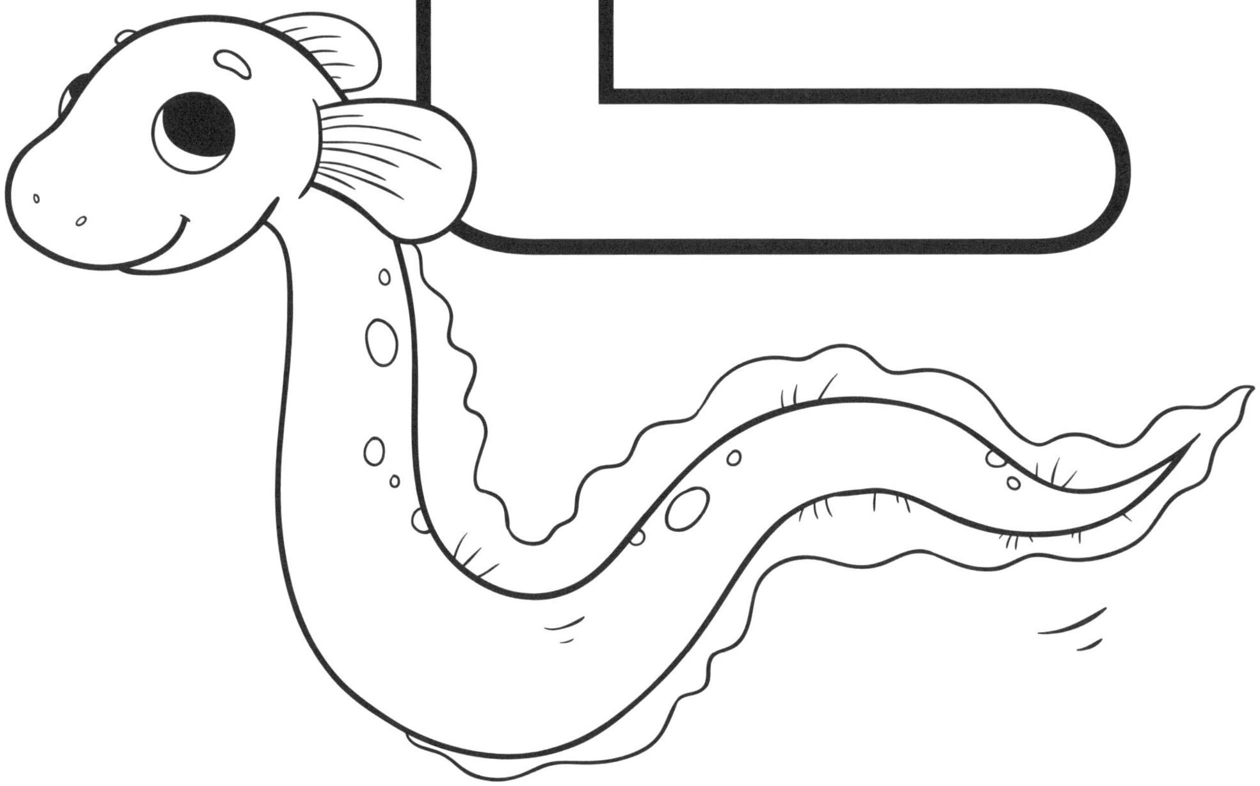

Eel

F

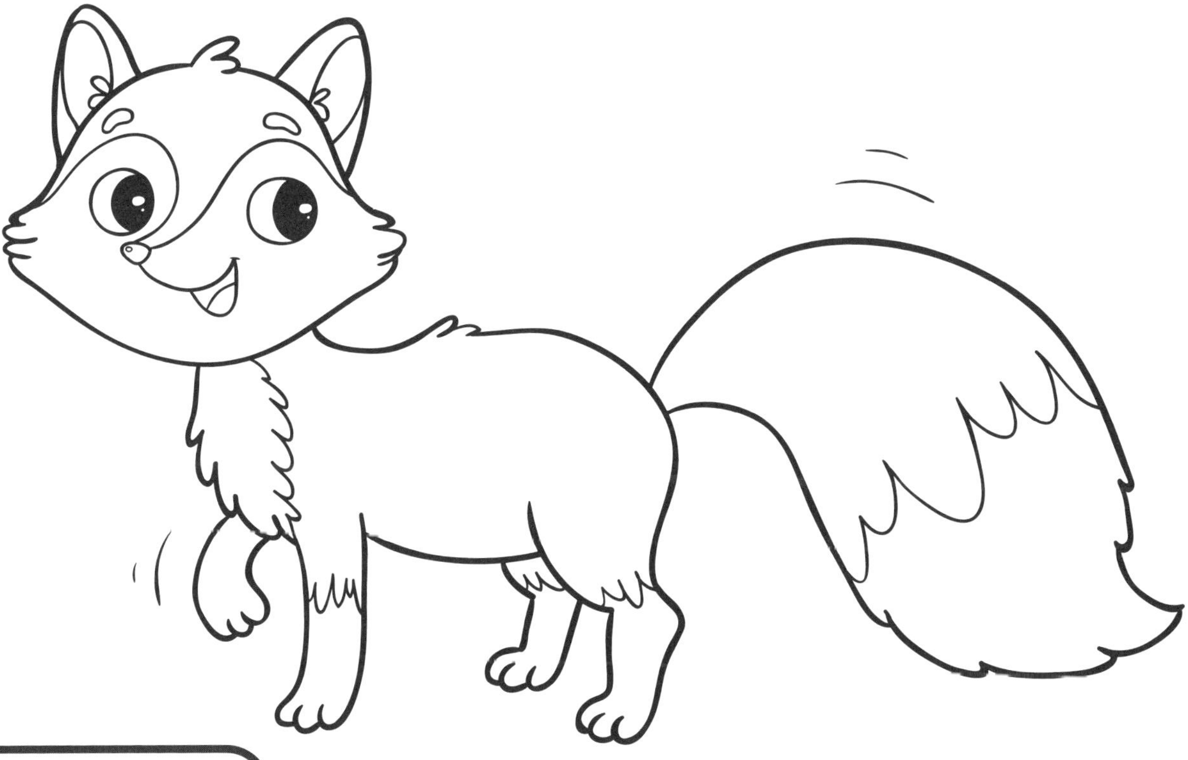

Fox

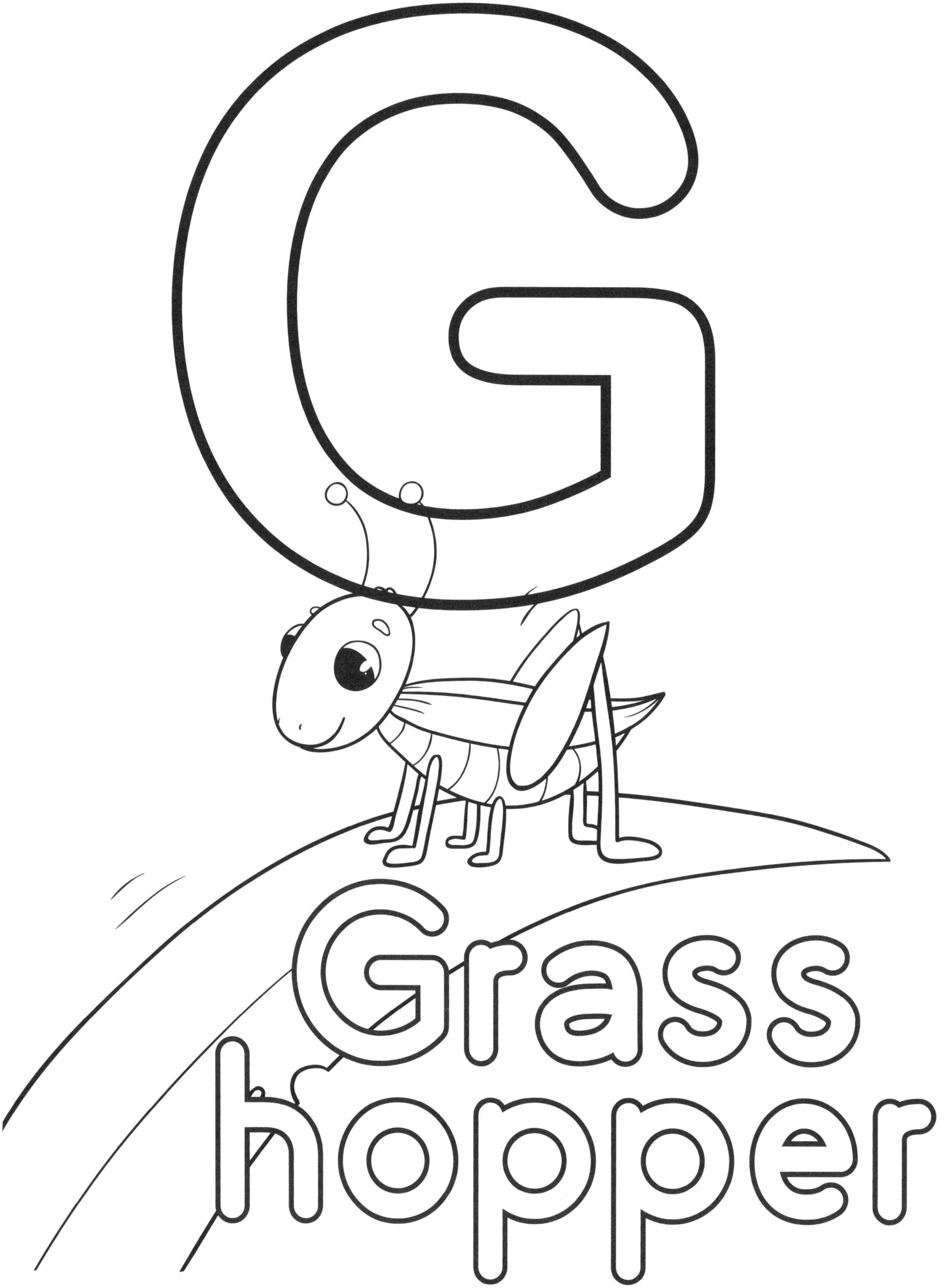
G
Grass
hopper

H

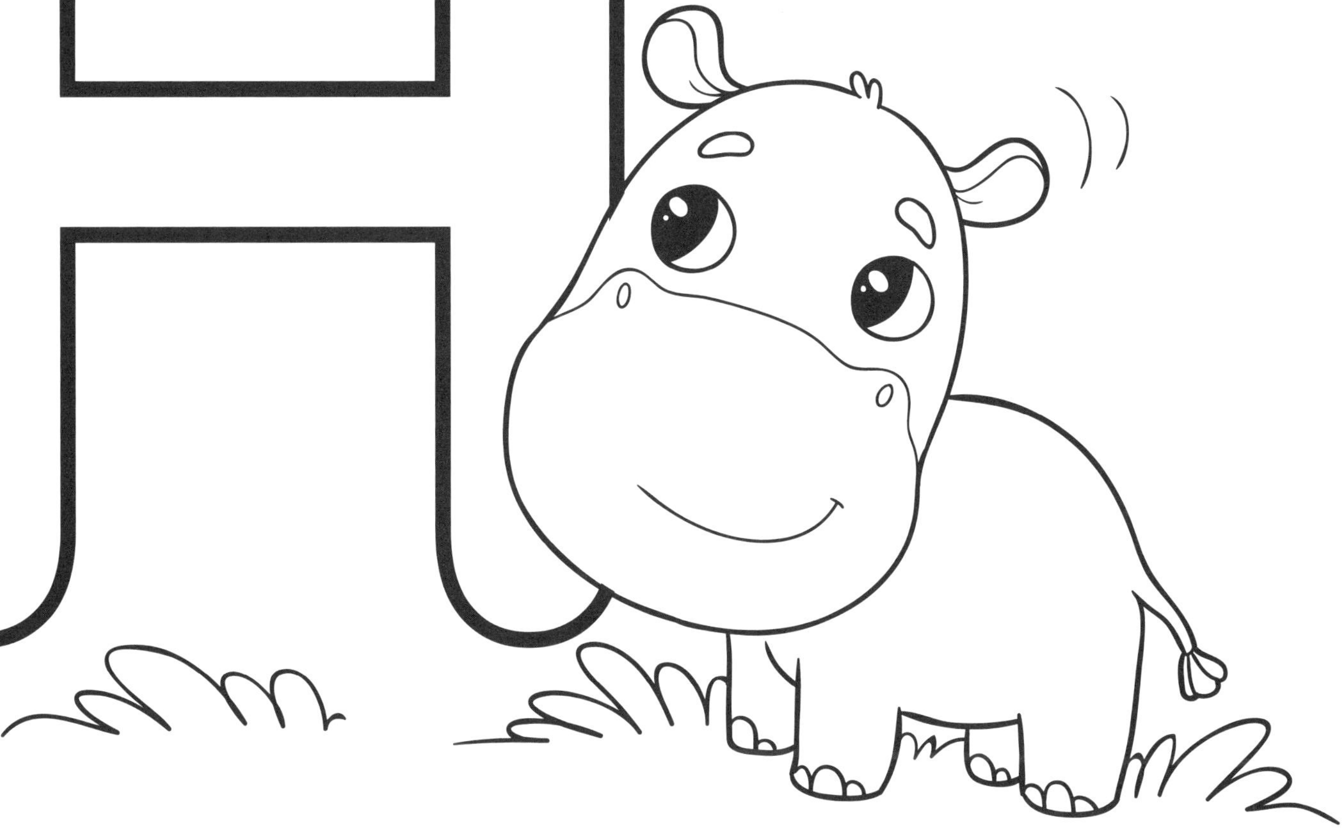

Hippo

I

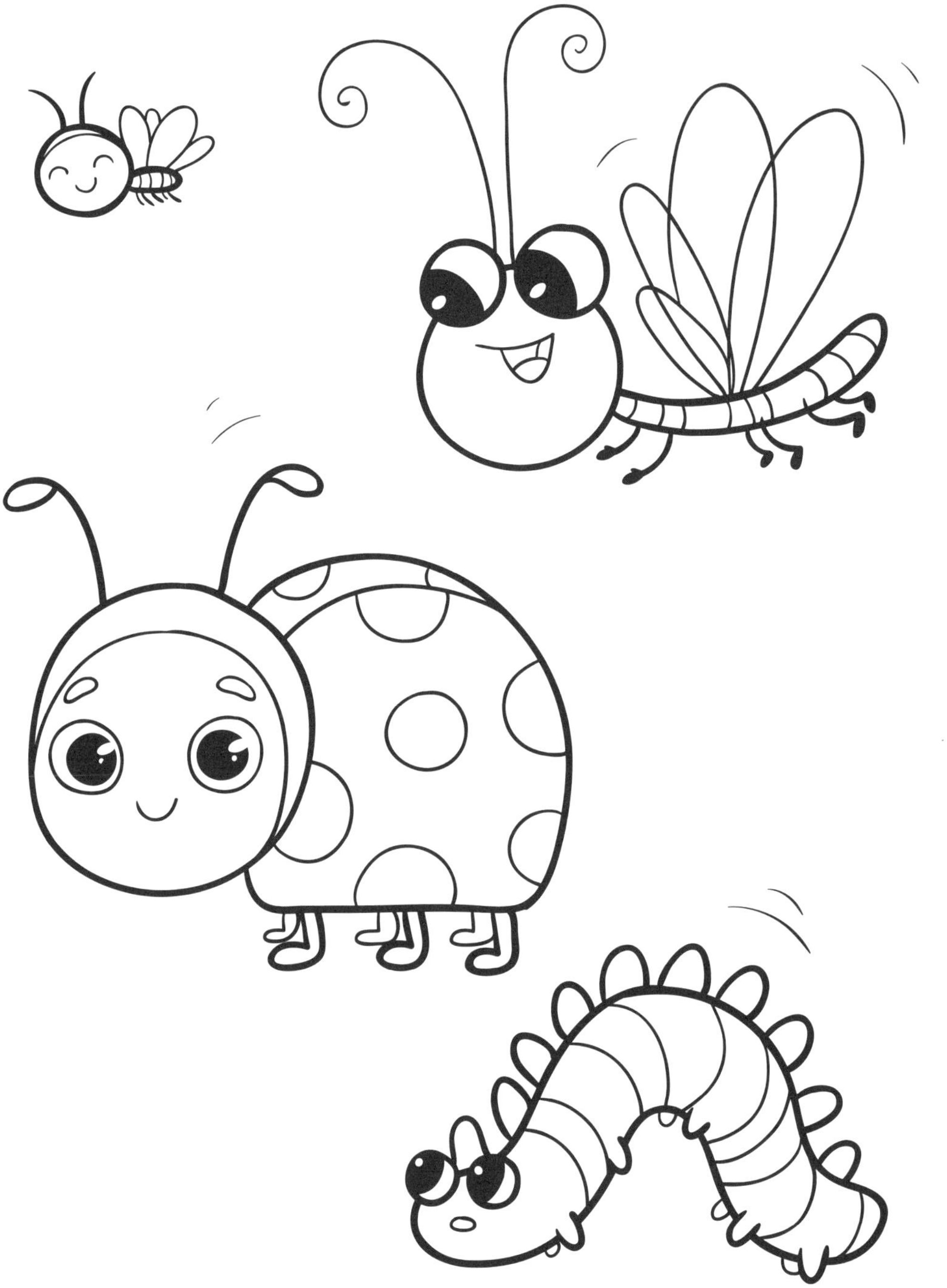

Insect

J

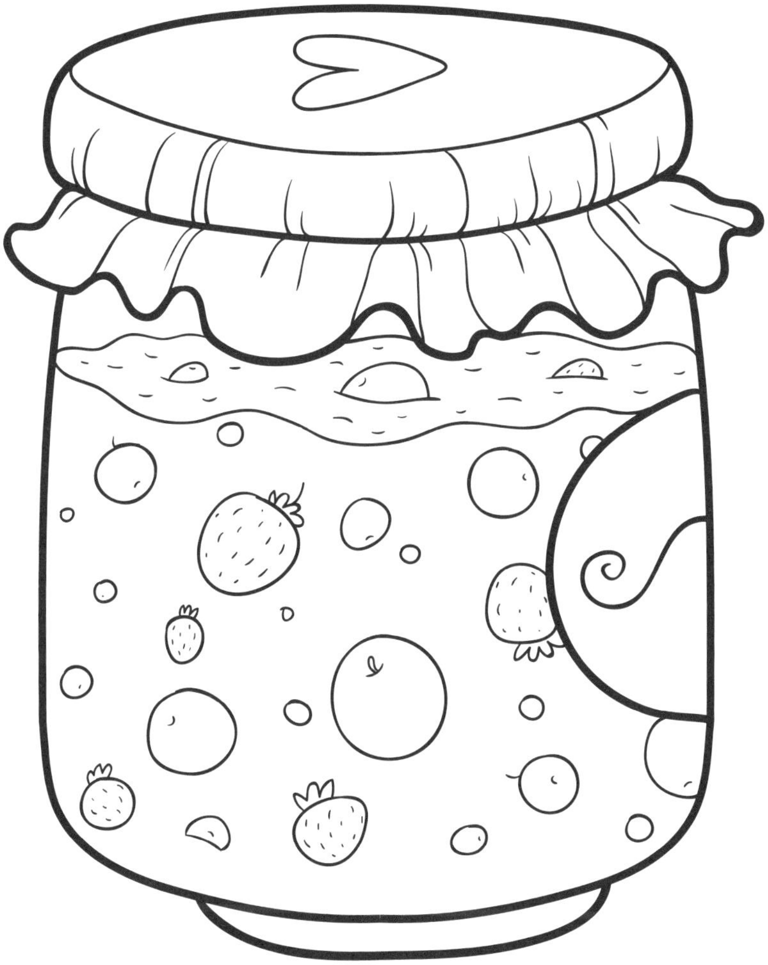

Jam

K

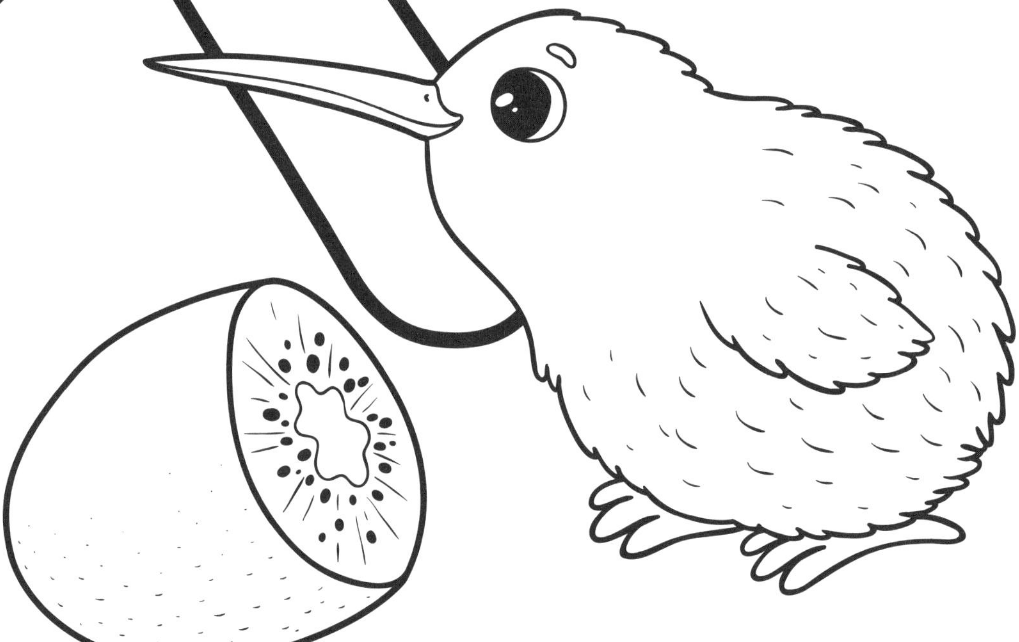

Kiwi

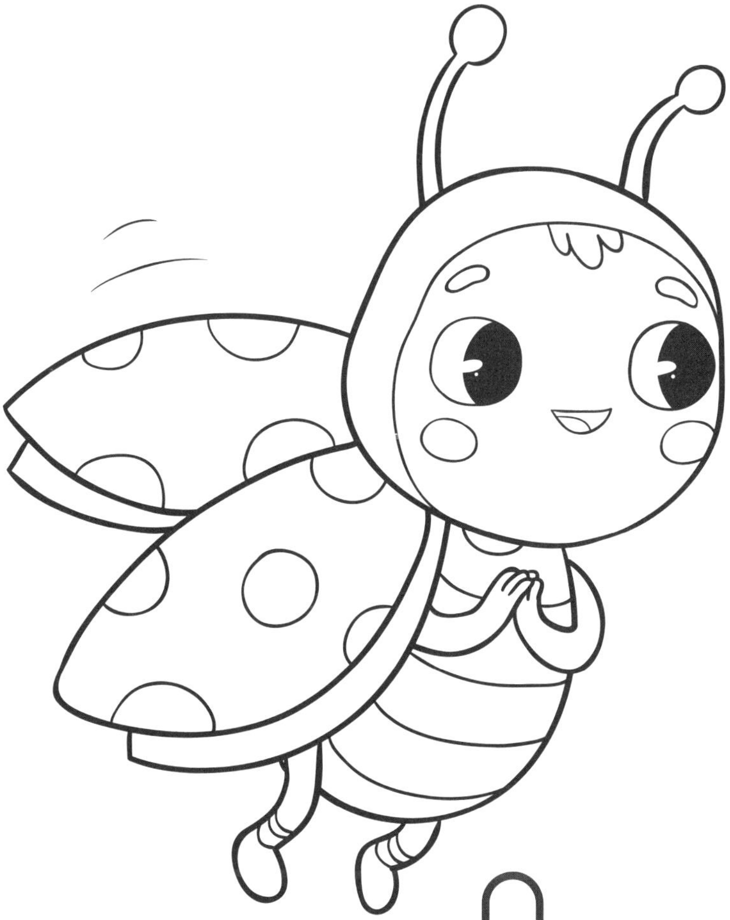

L

Lady bug

M

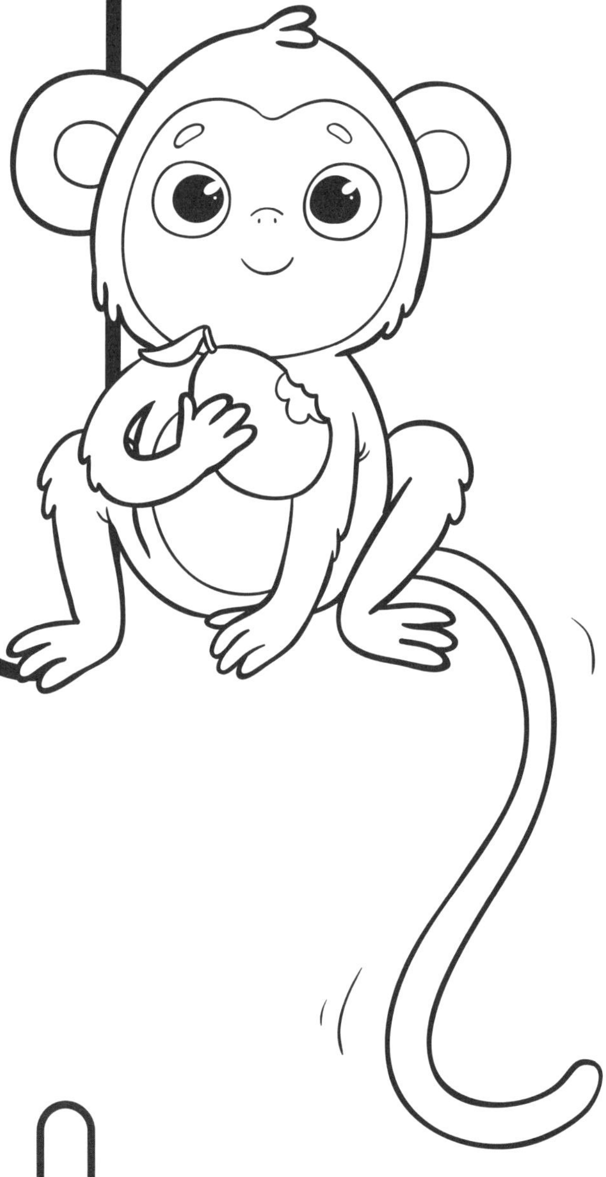

Monkey

N

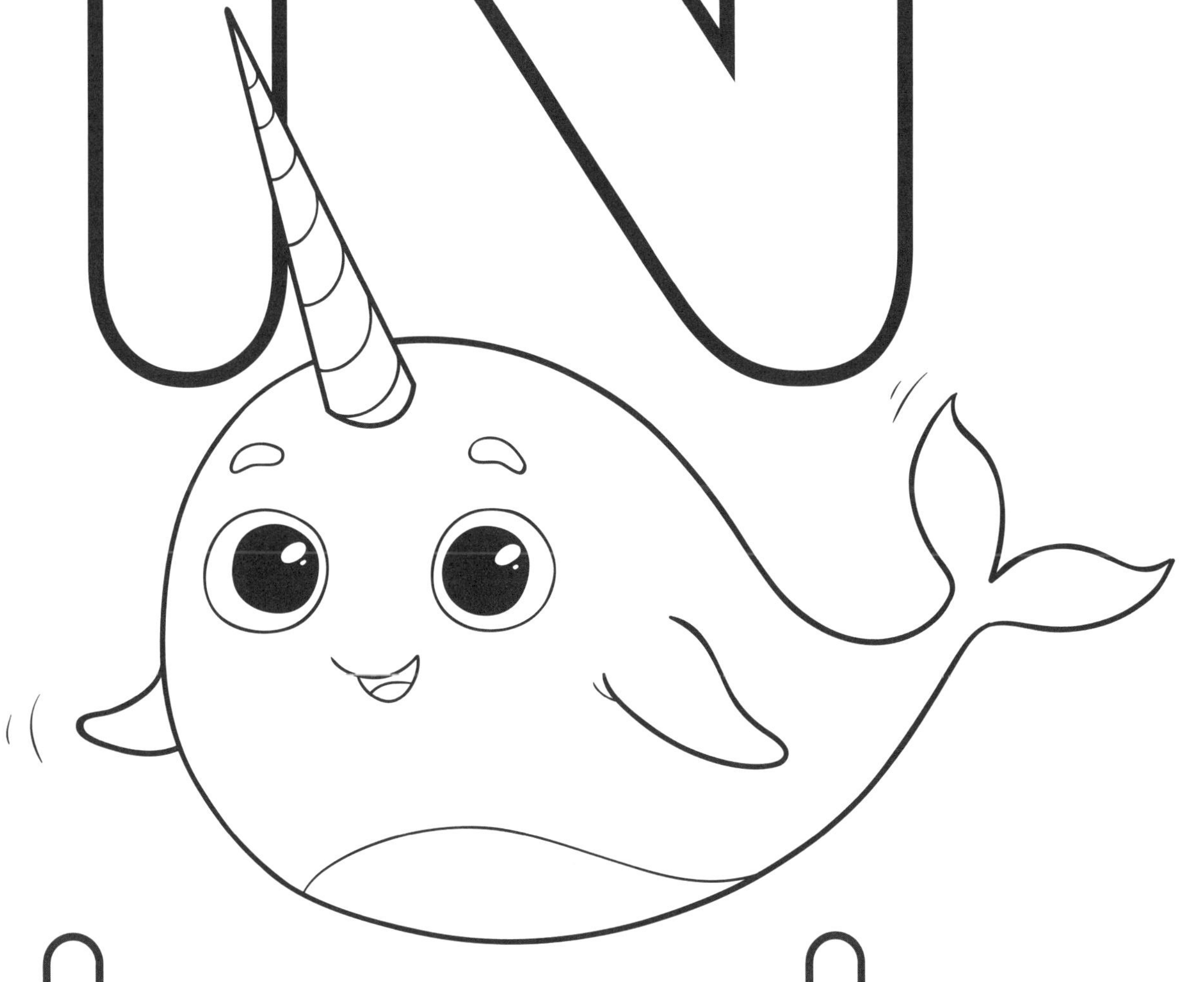

Narwhal

O

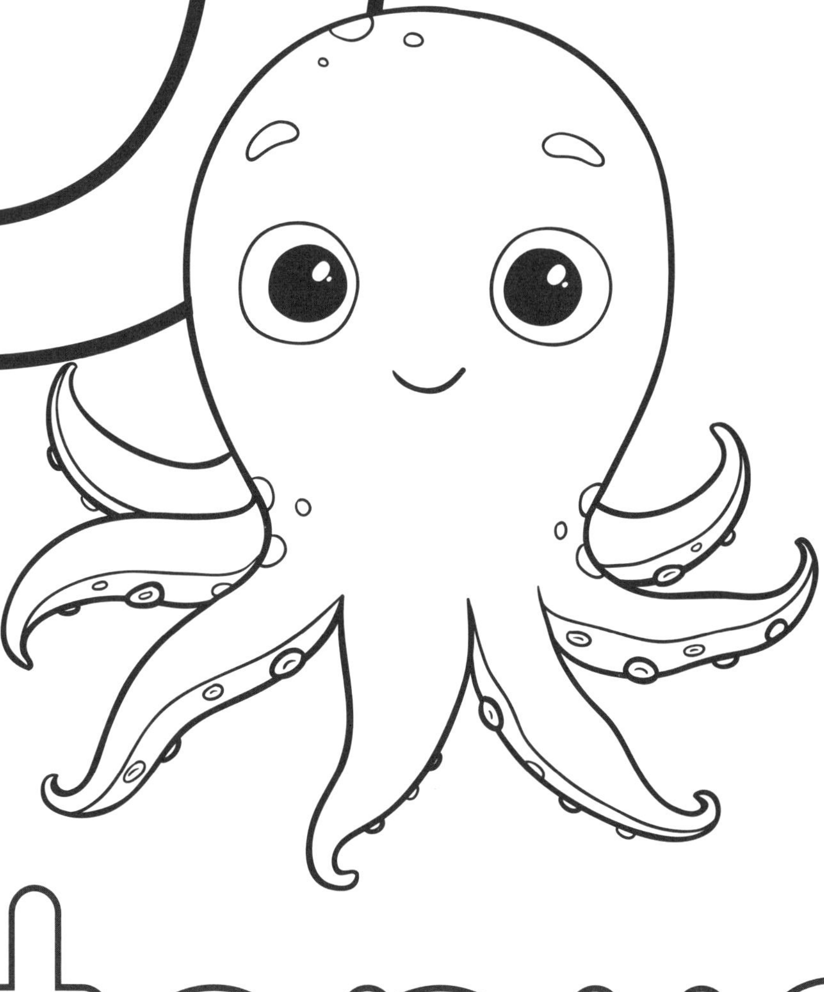

Octopus

P

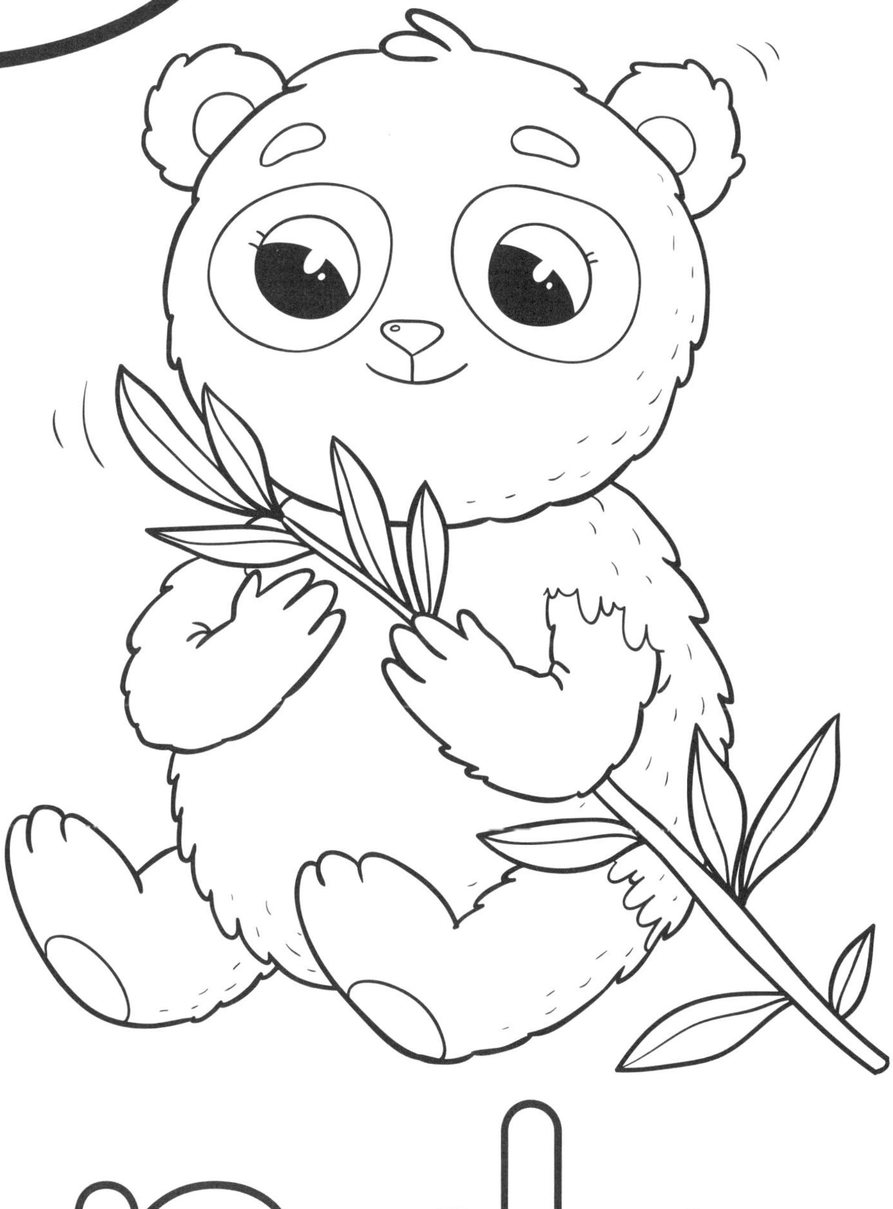

Panda

Q

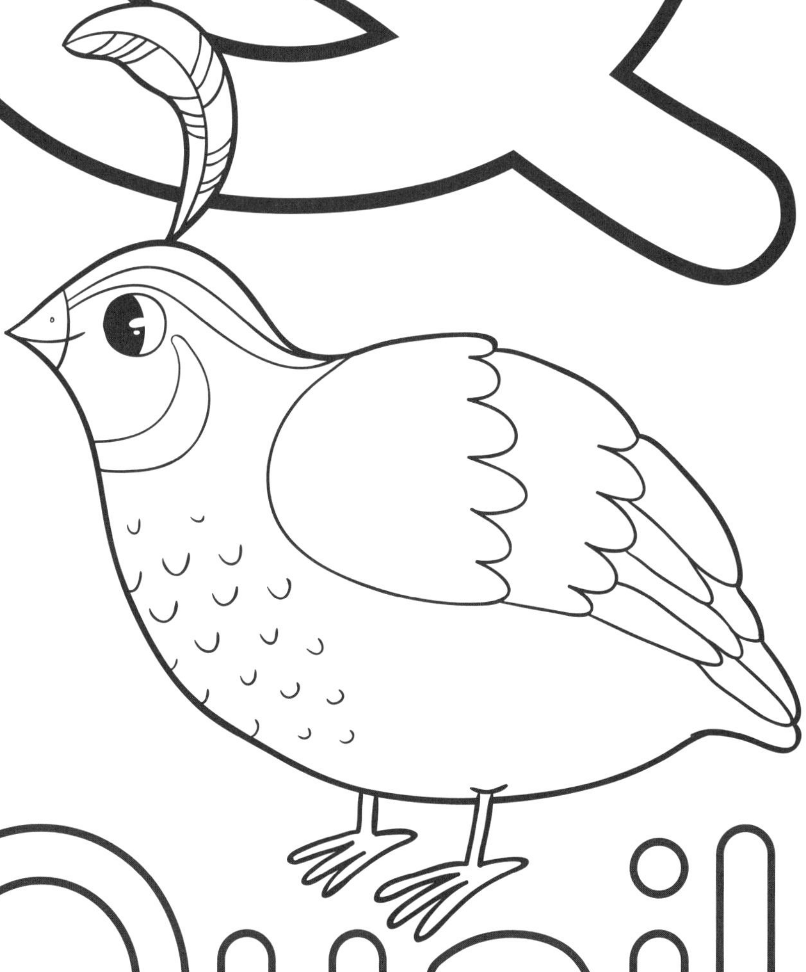

Quail

R

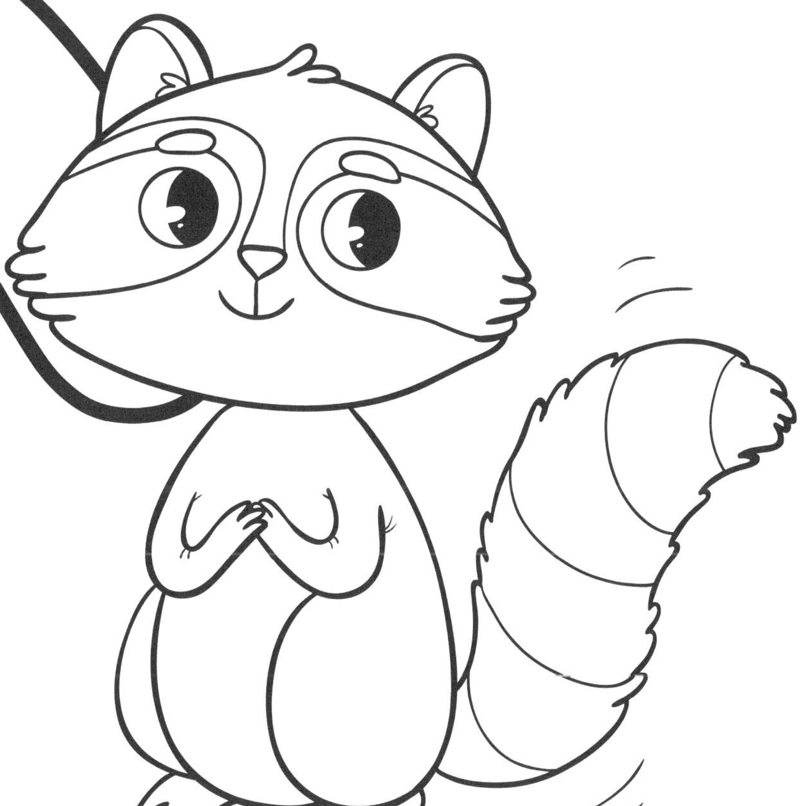

Racoon

S

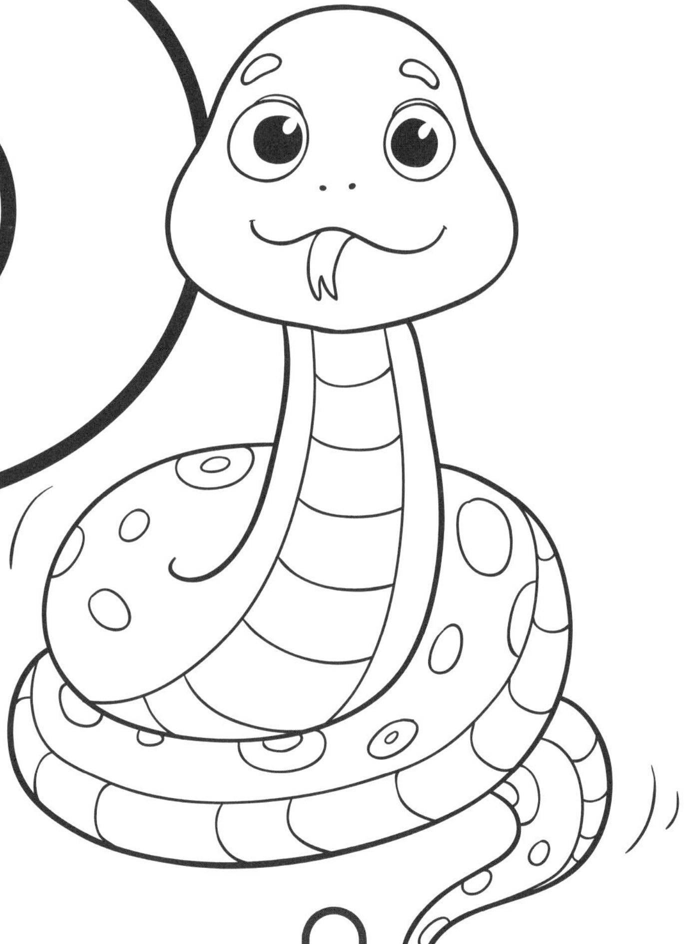

Snake

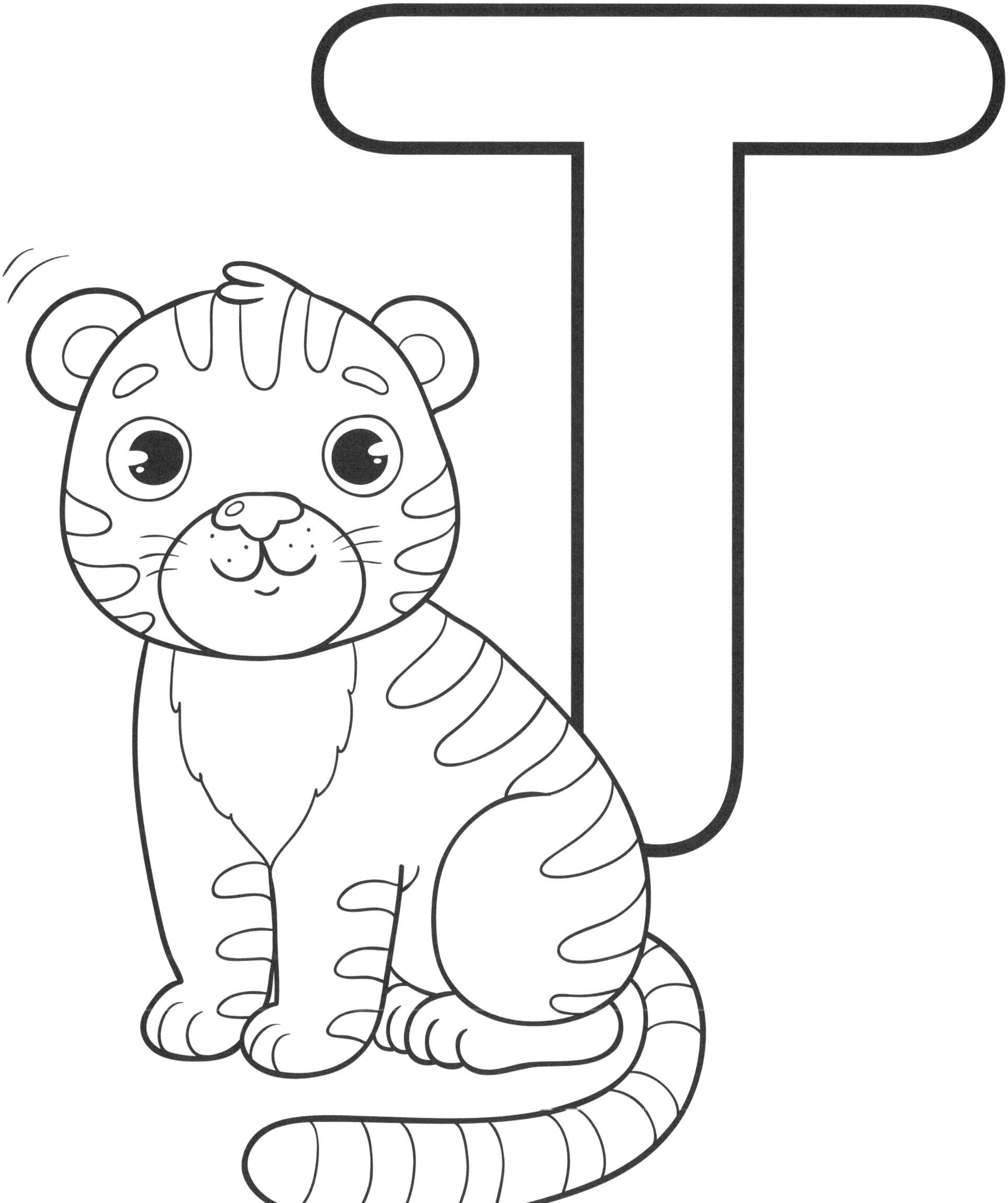

Tiger

U

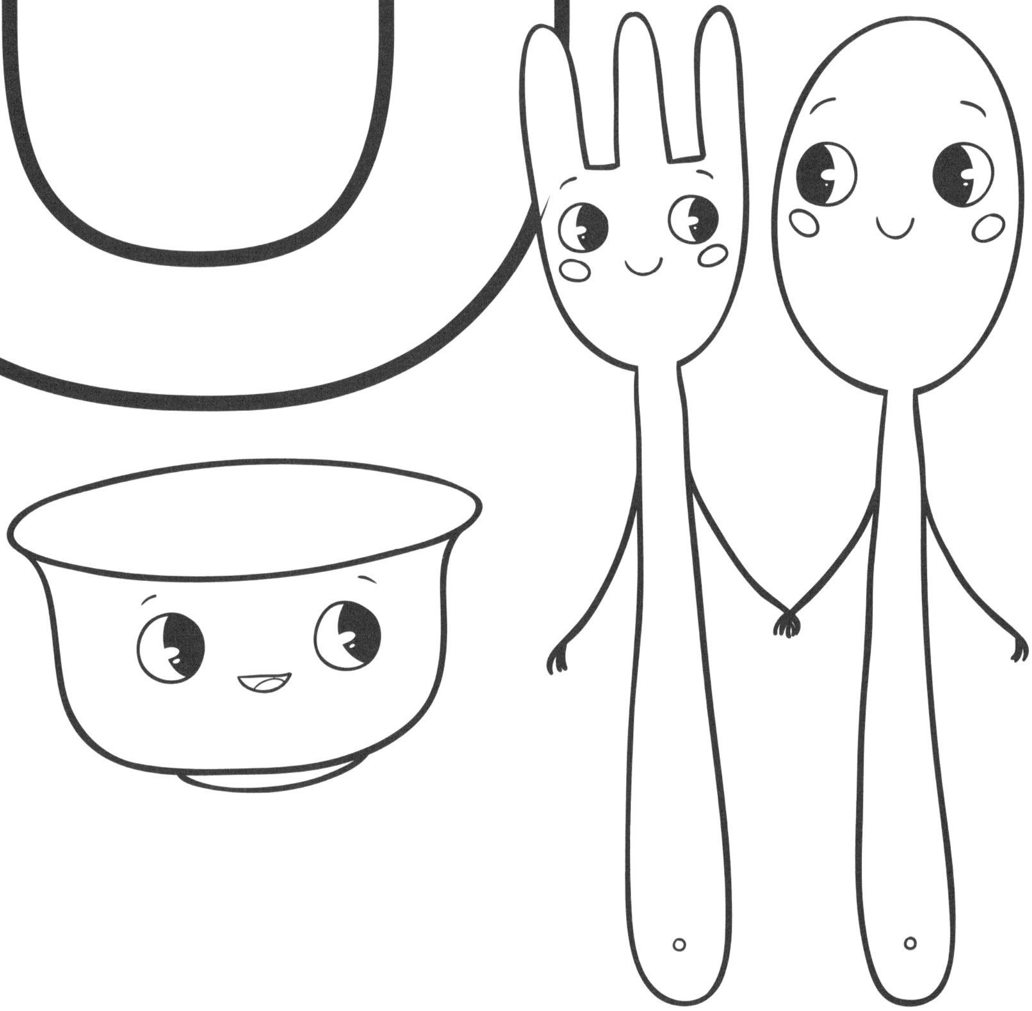

Utensils

V

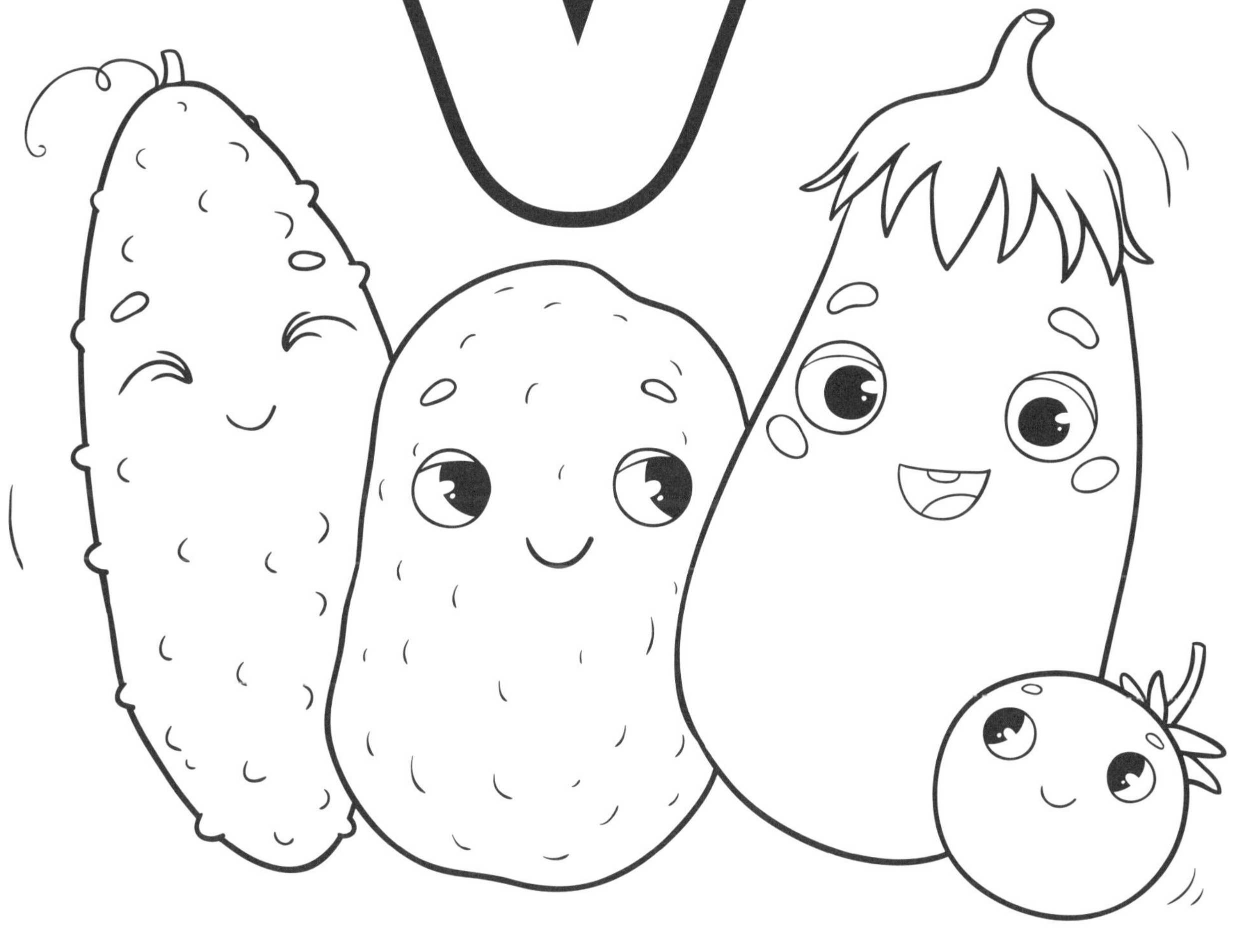

Vegetables

W

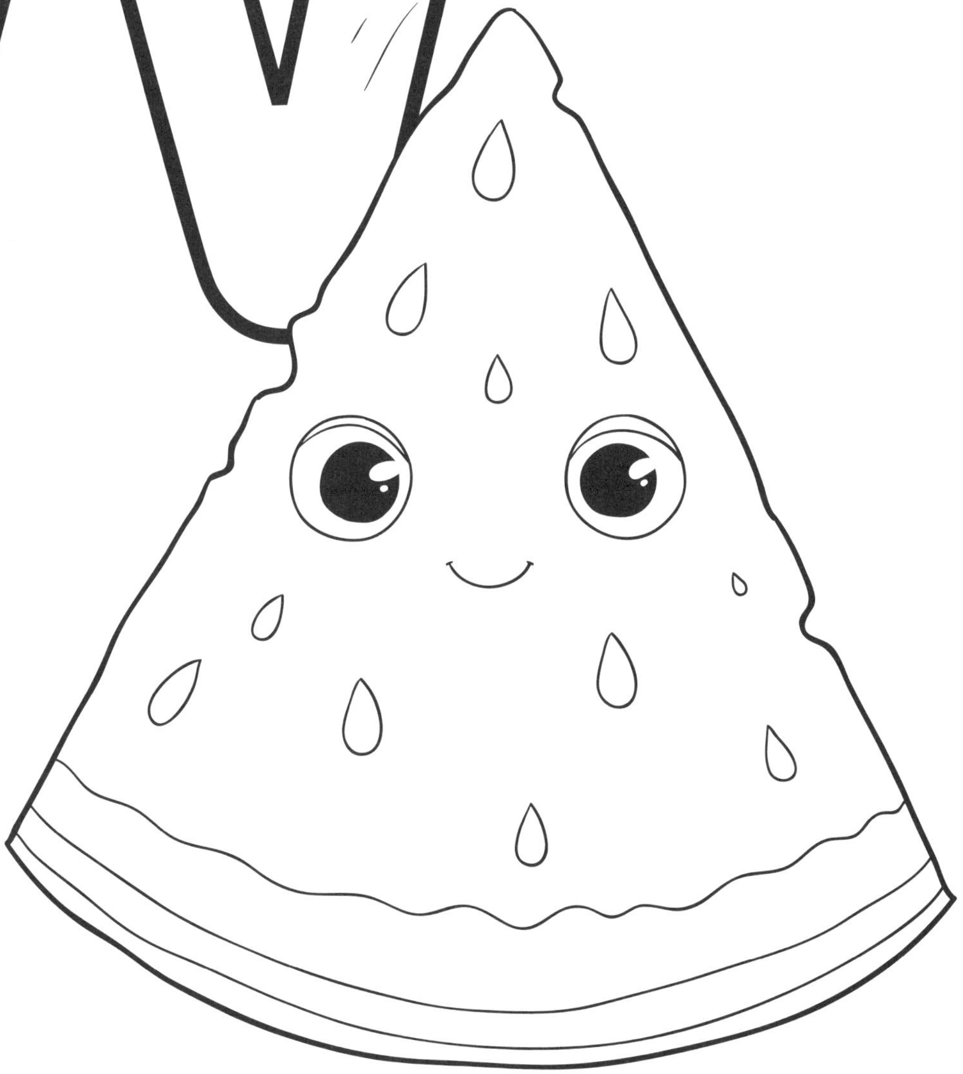

Watermelon

X

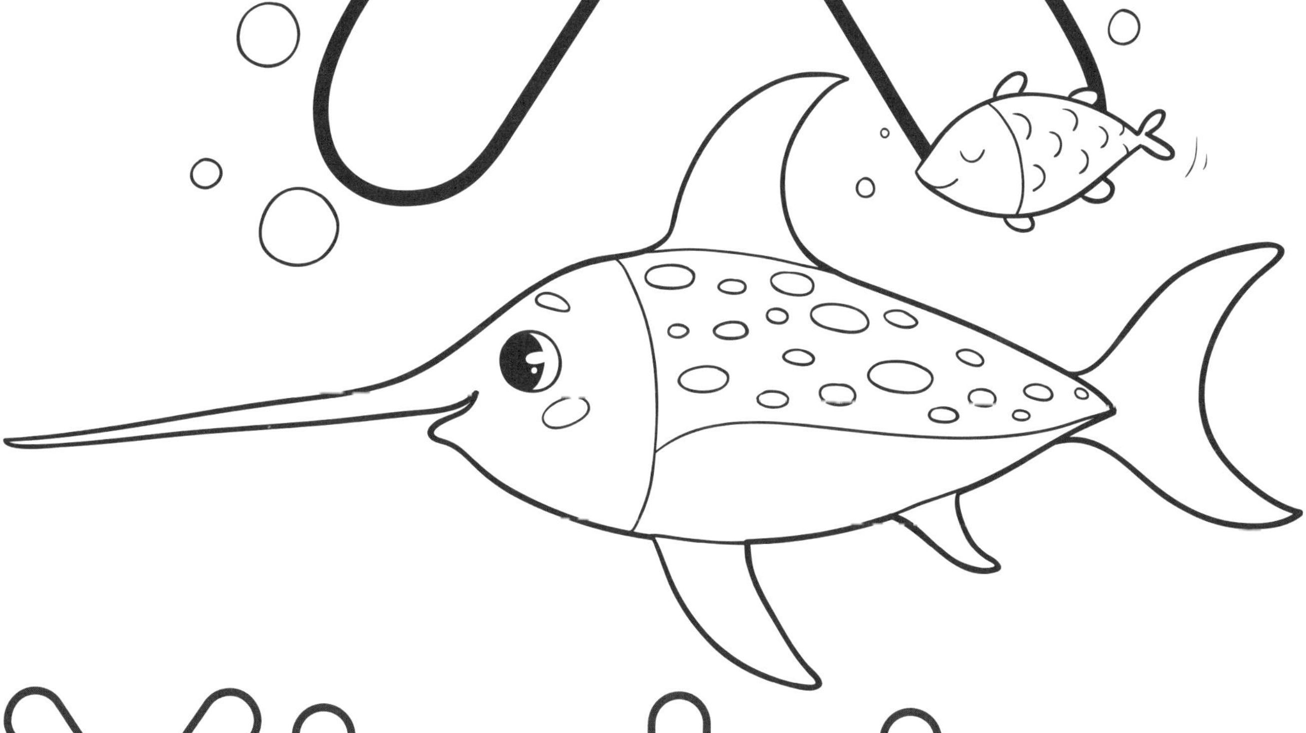

Xiphias

Y

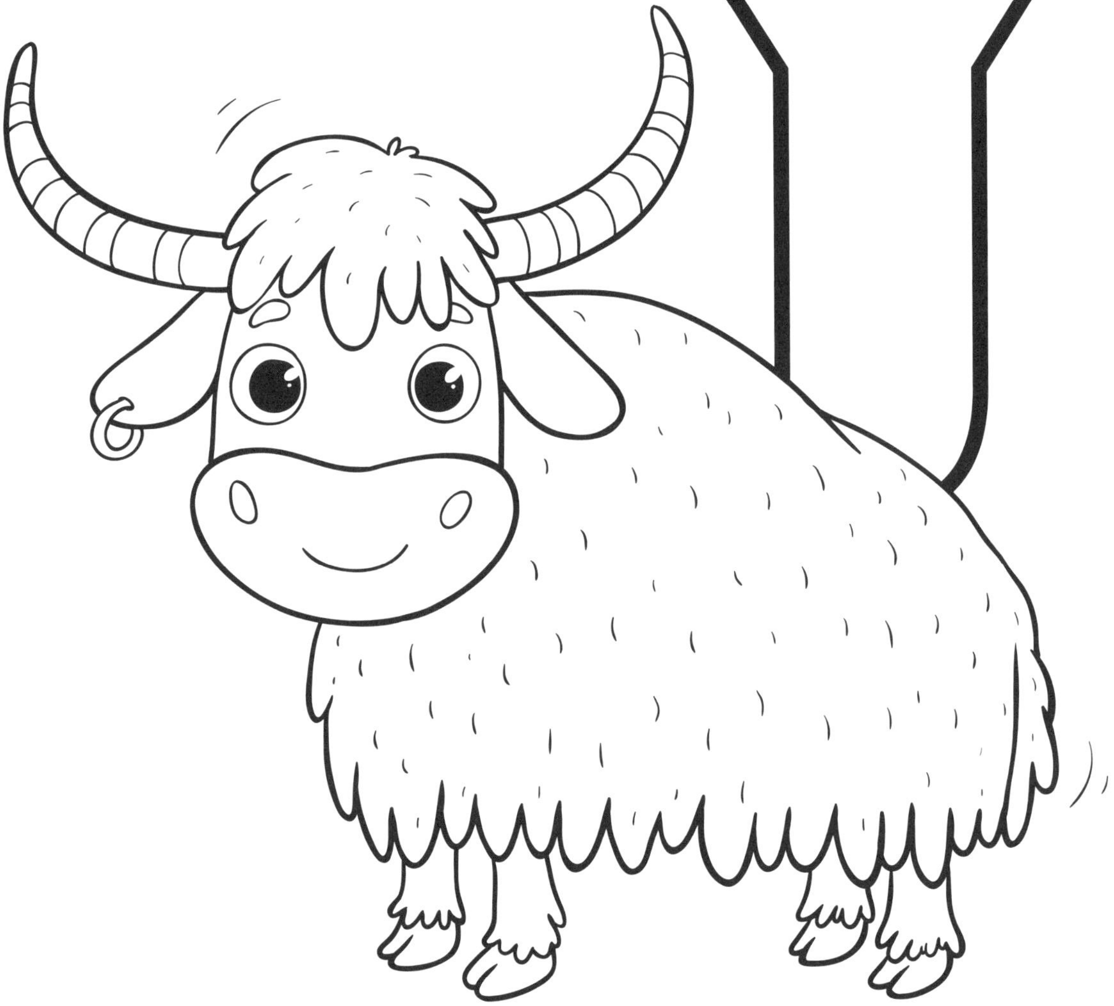

Yak

Z

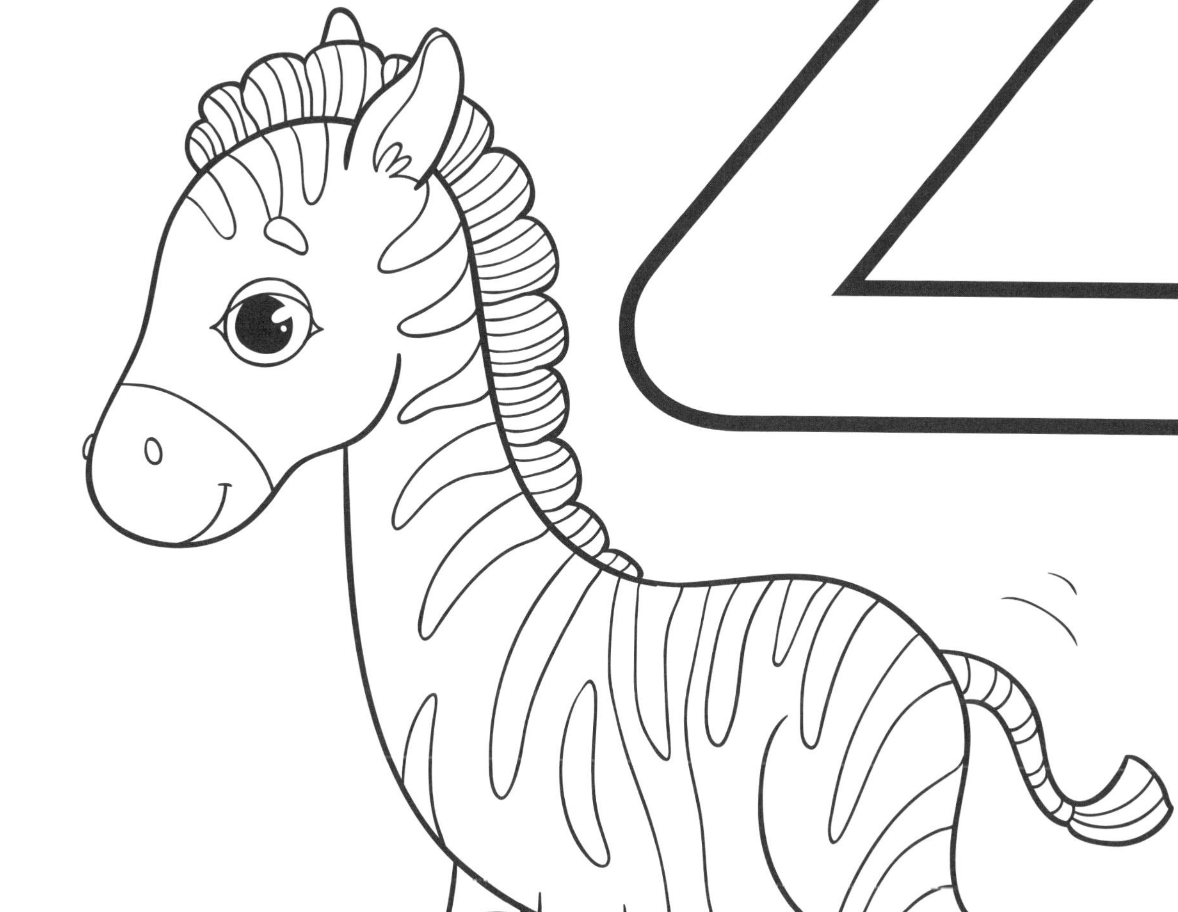

Zebra

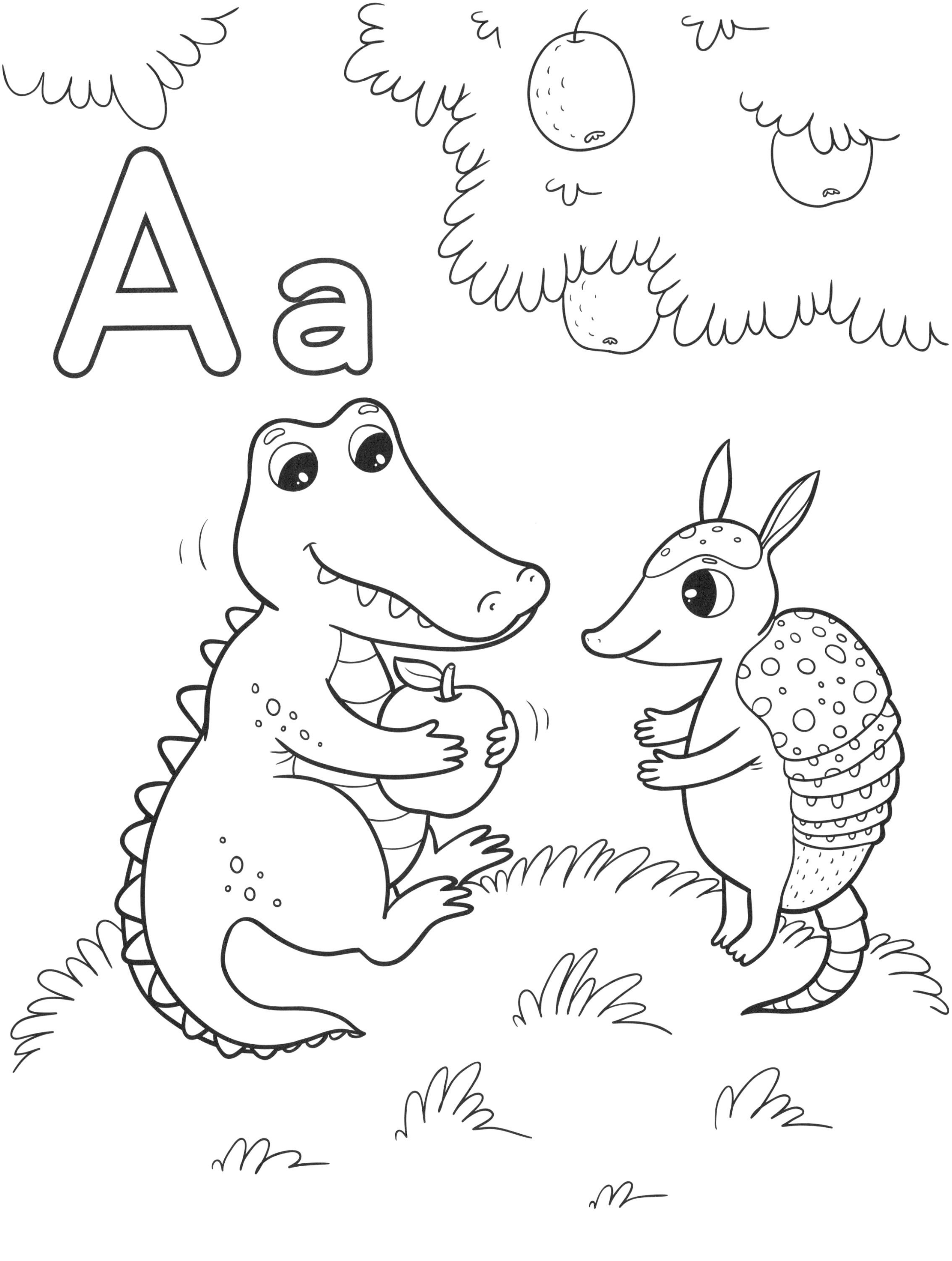
A a

B b

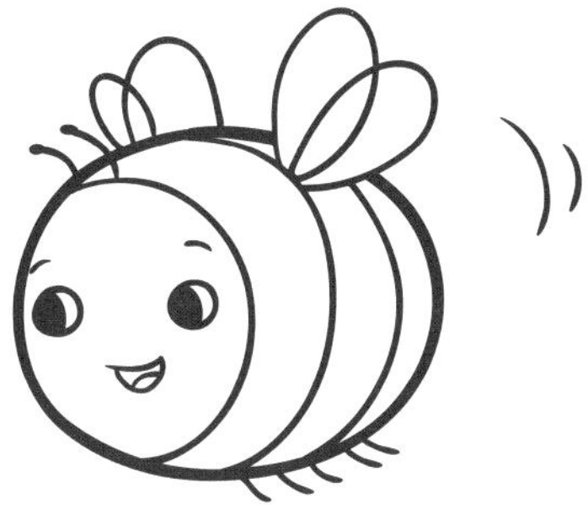

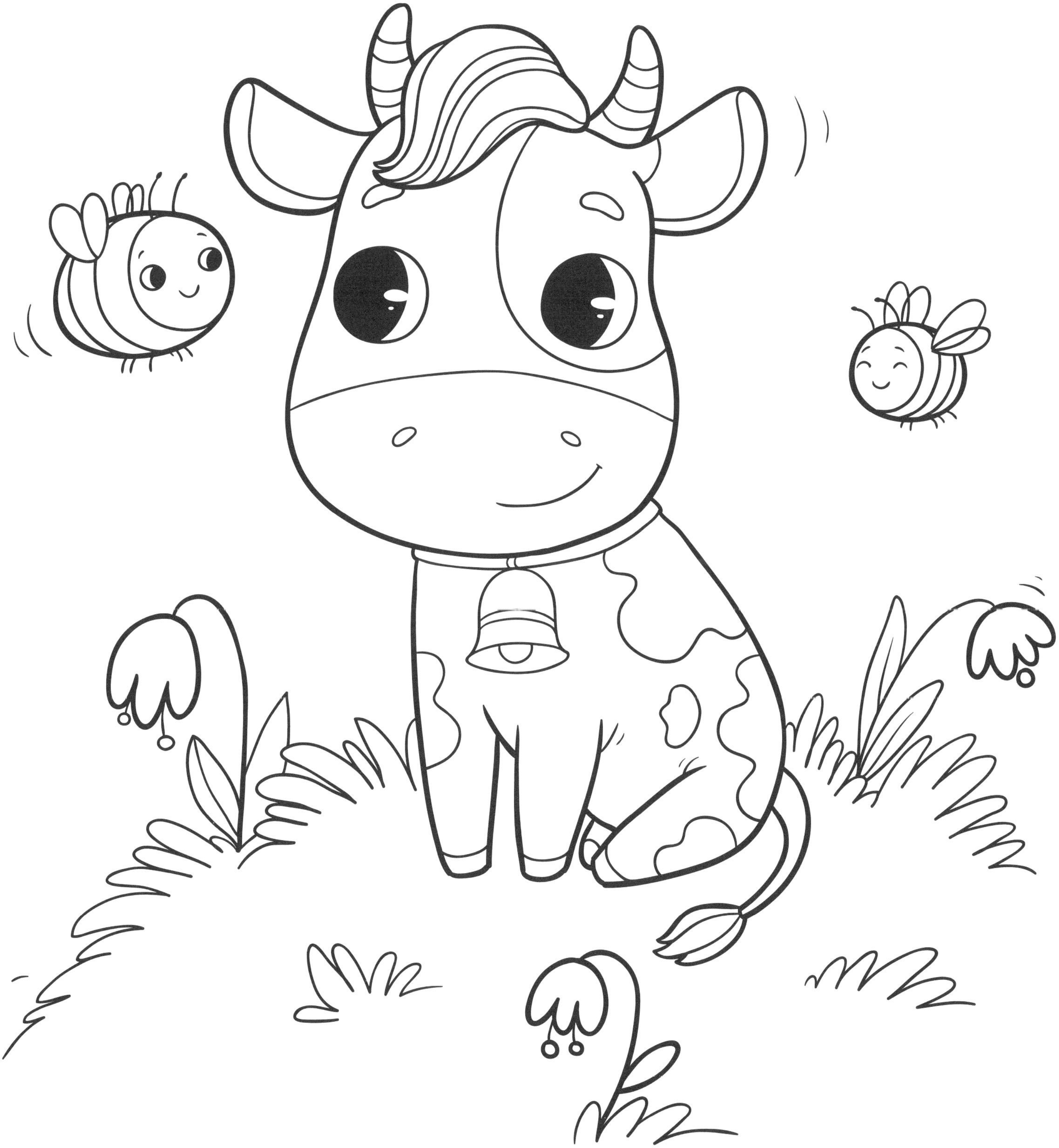

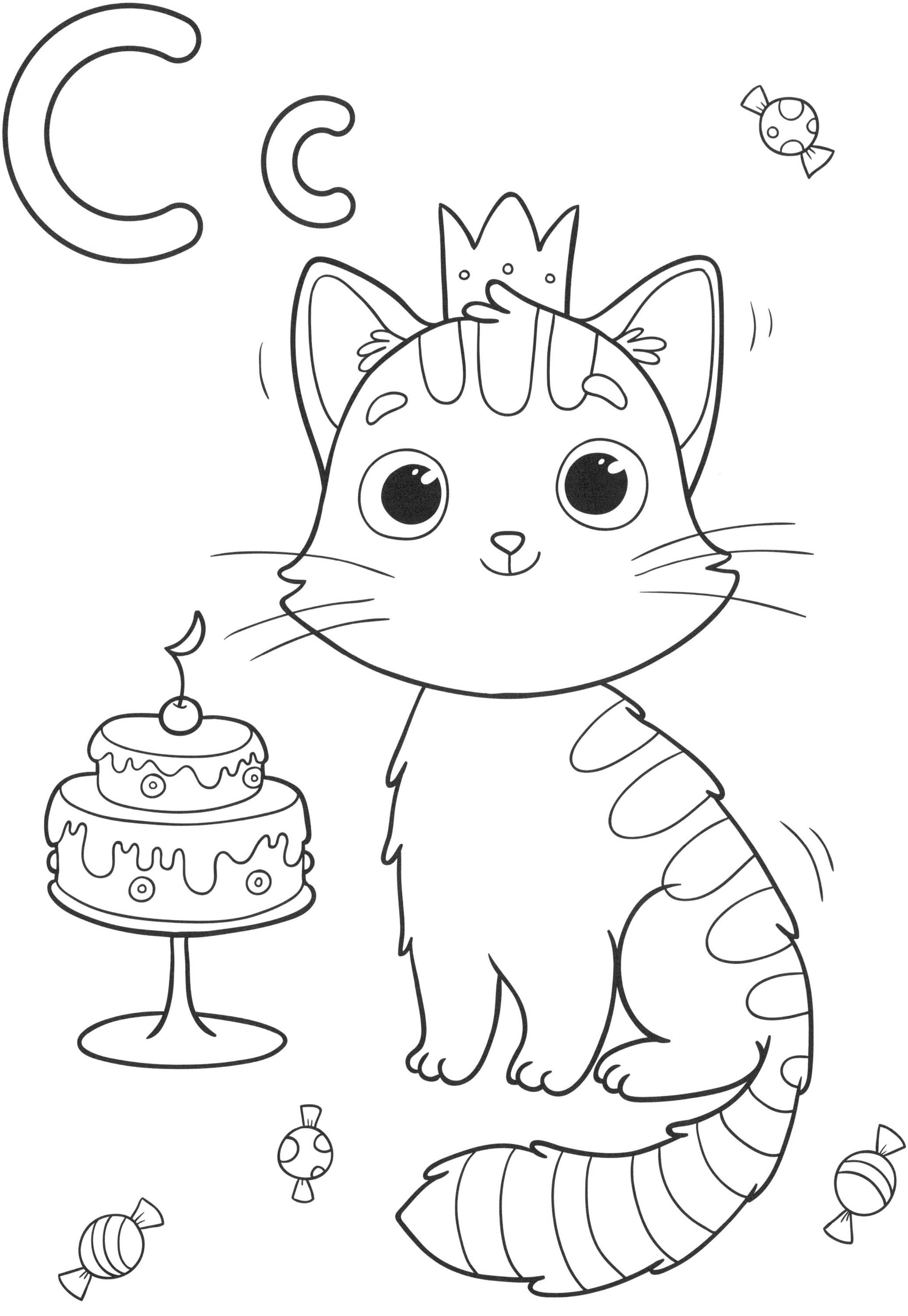
C c

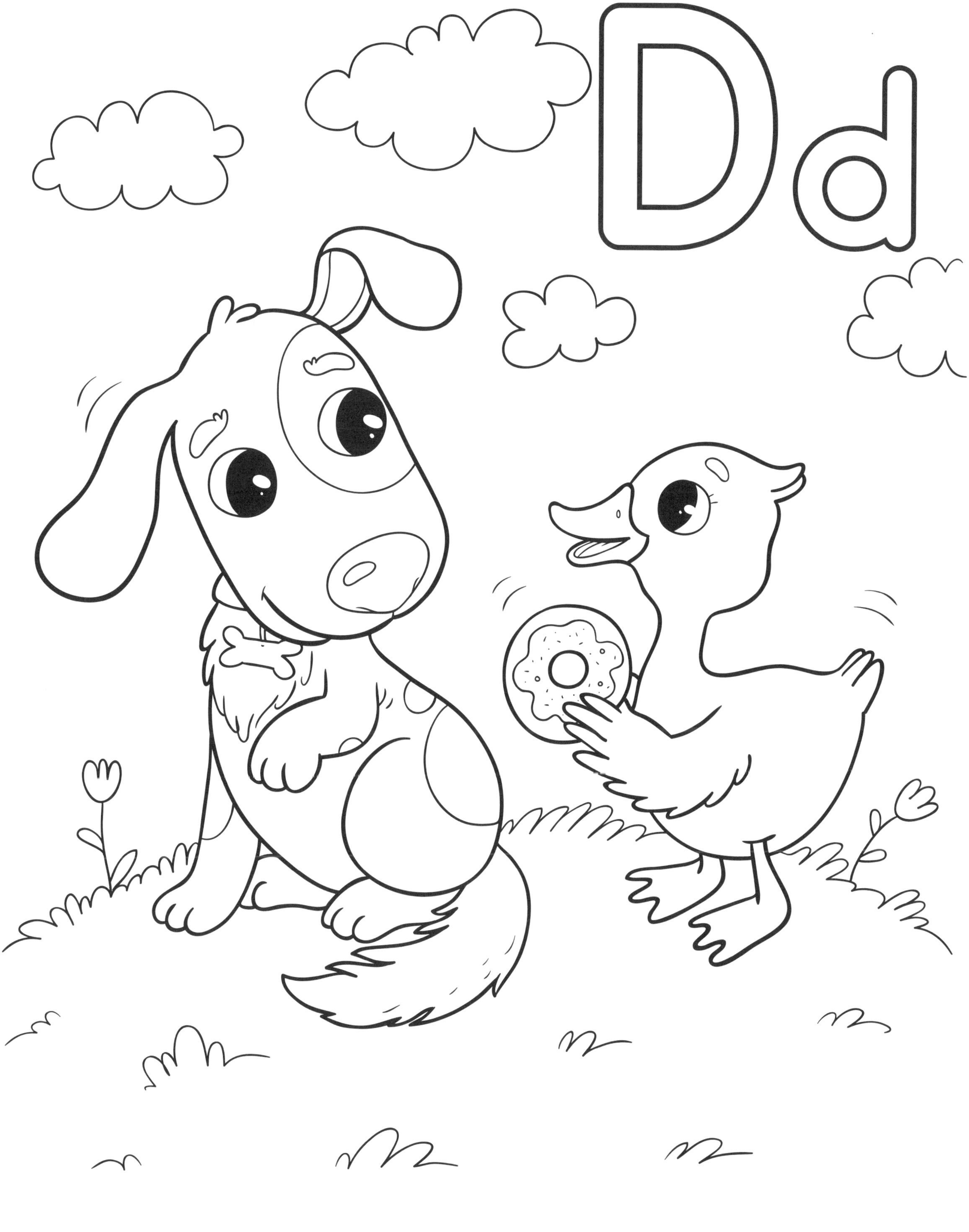
Dd

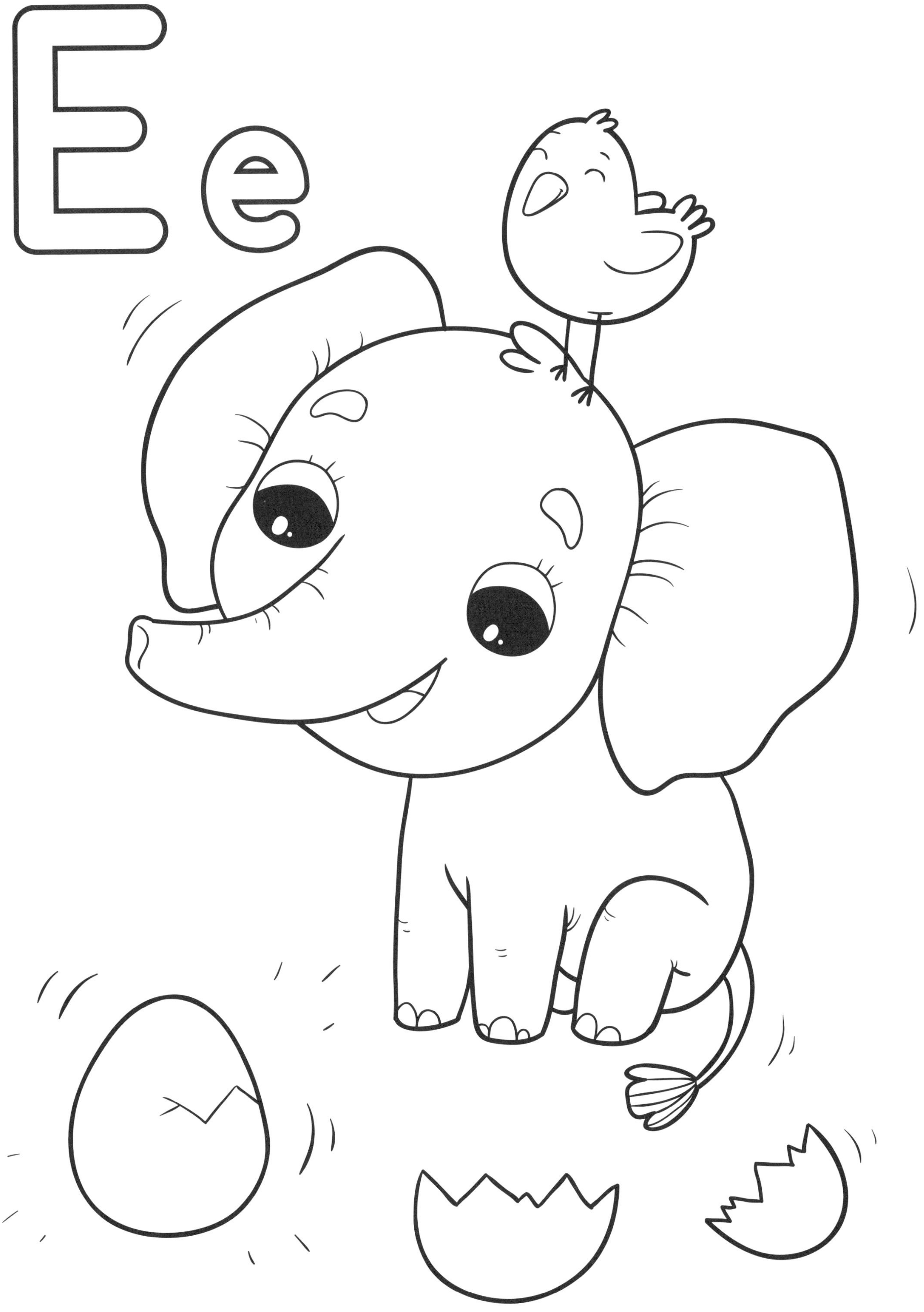
Ee

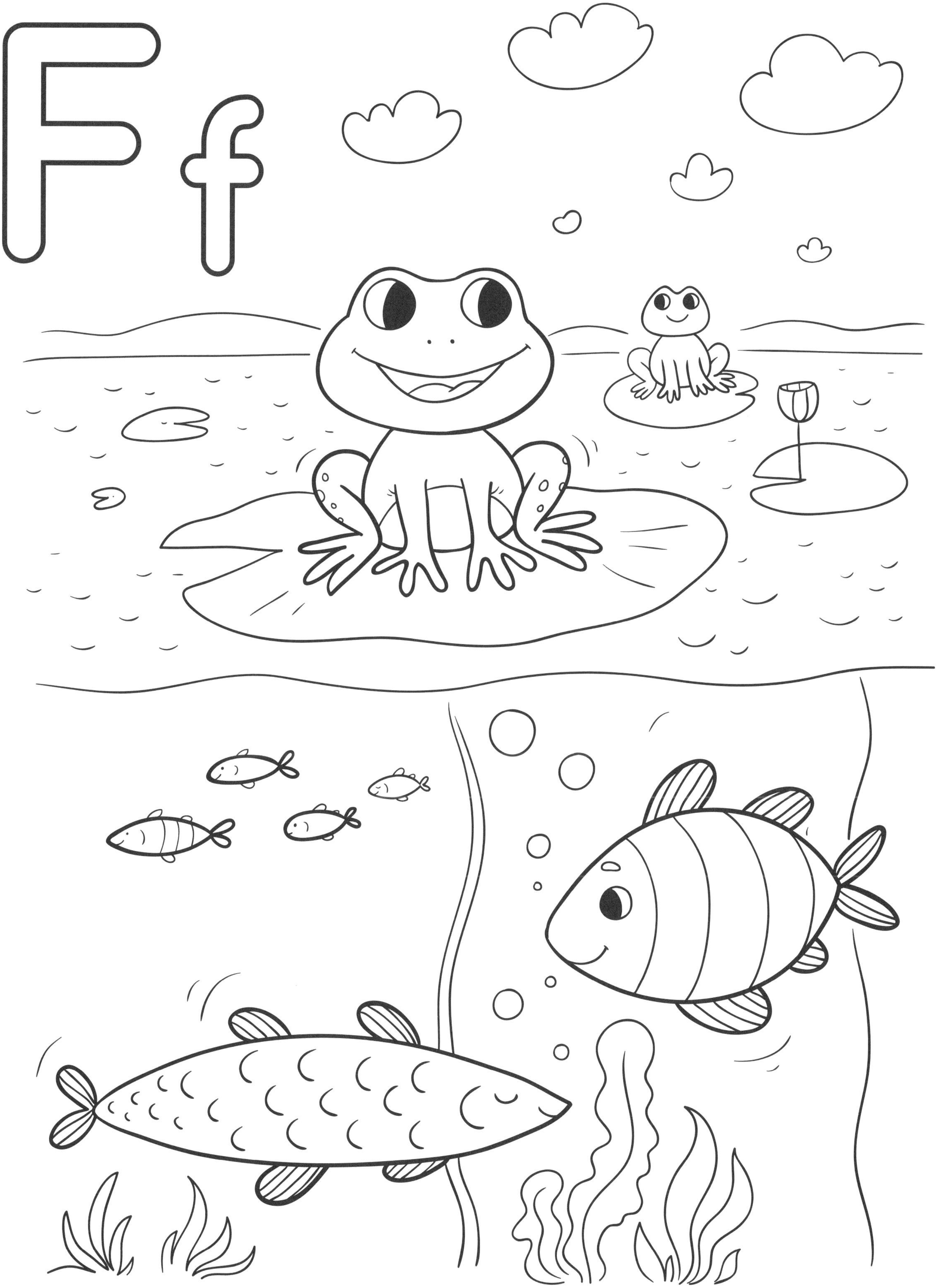

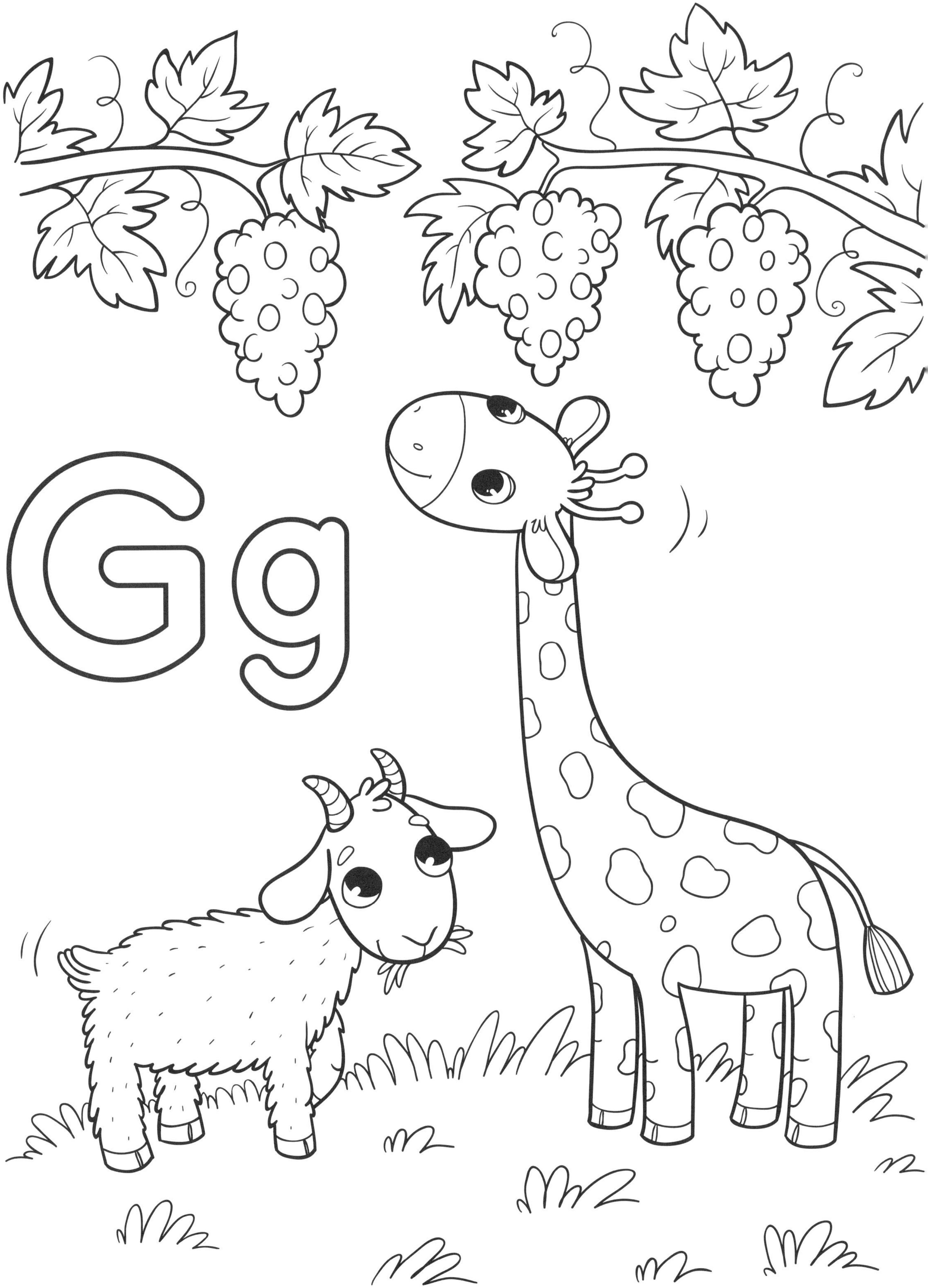
Gg

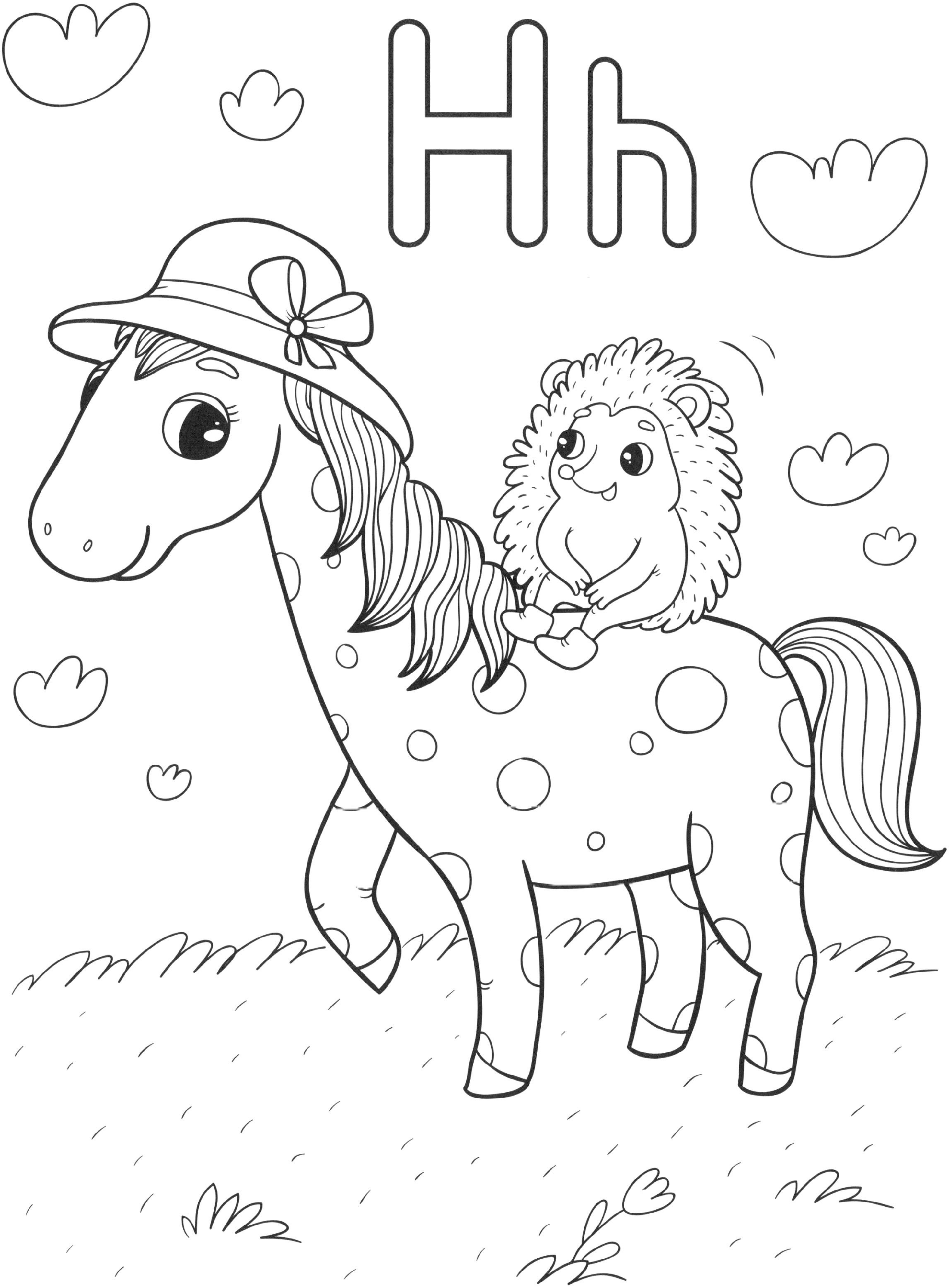
Hh

I i

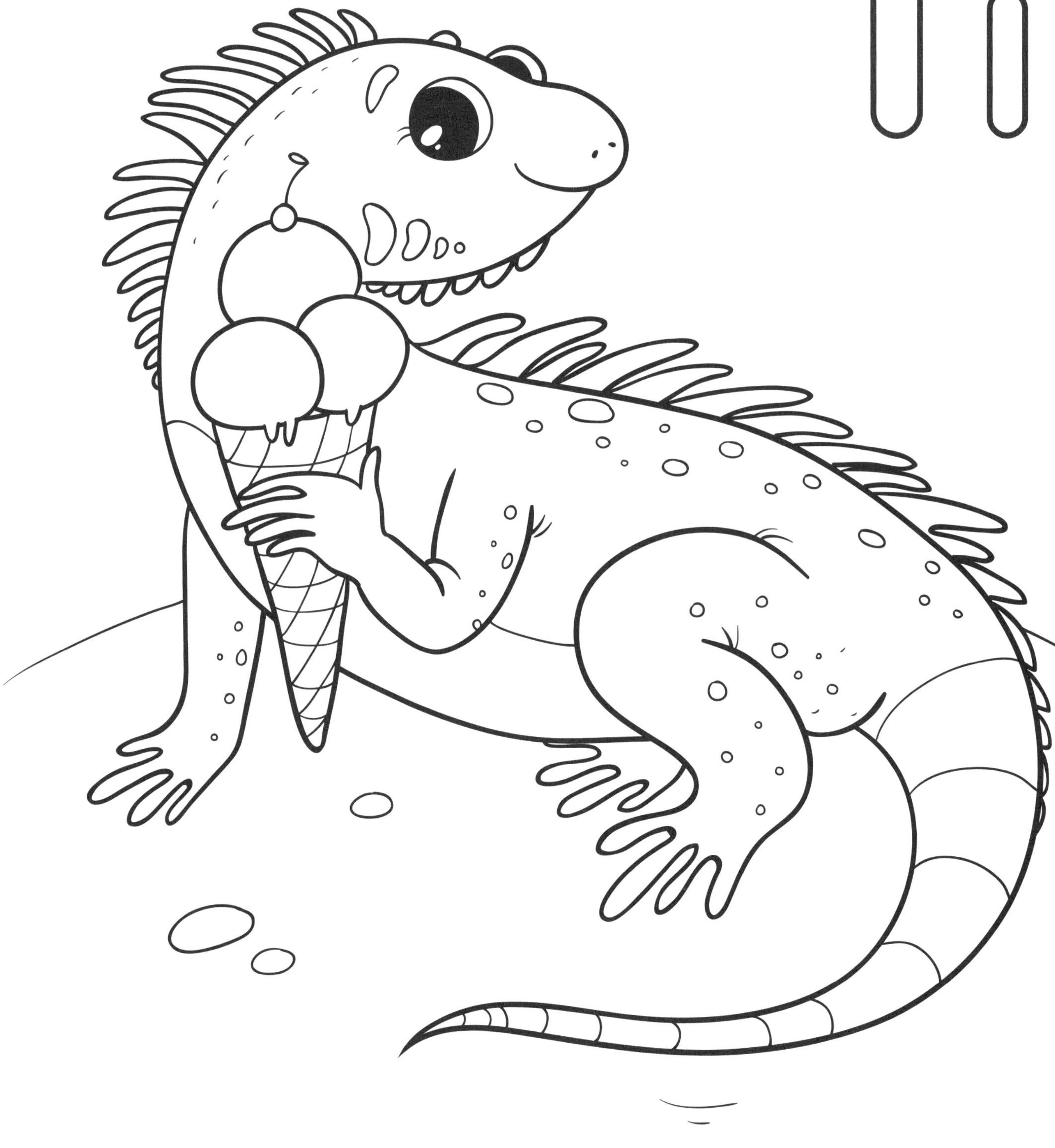

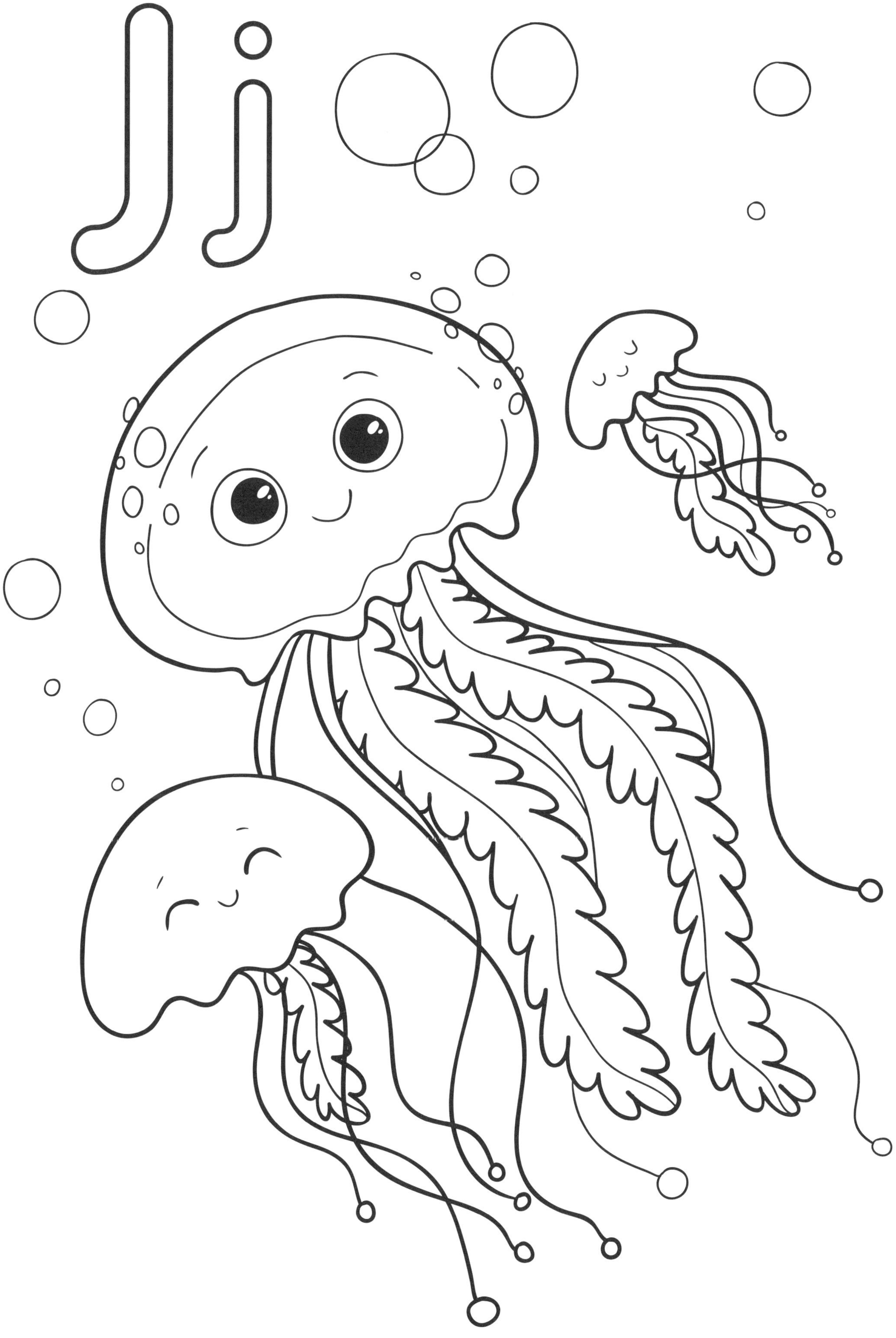
J j

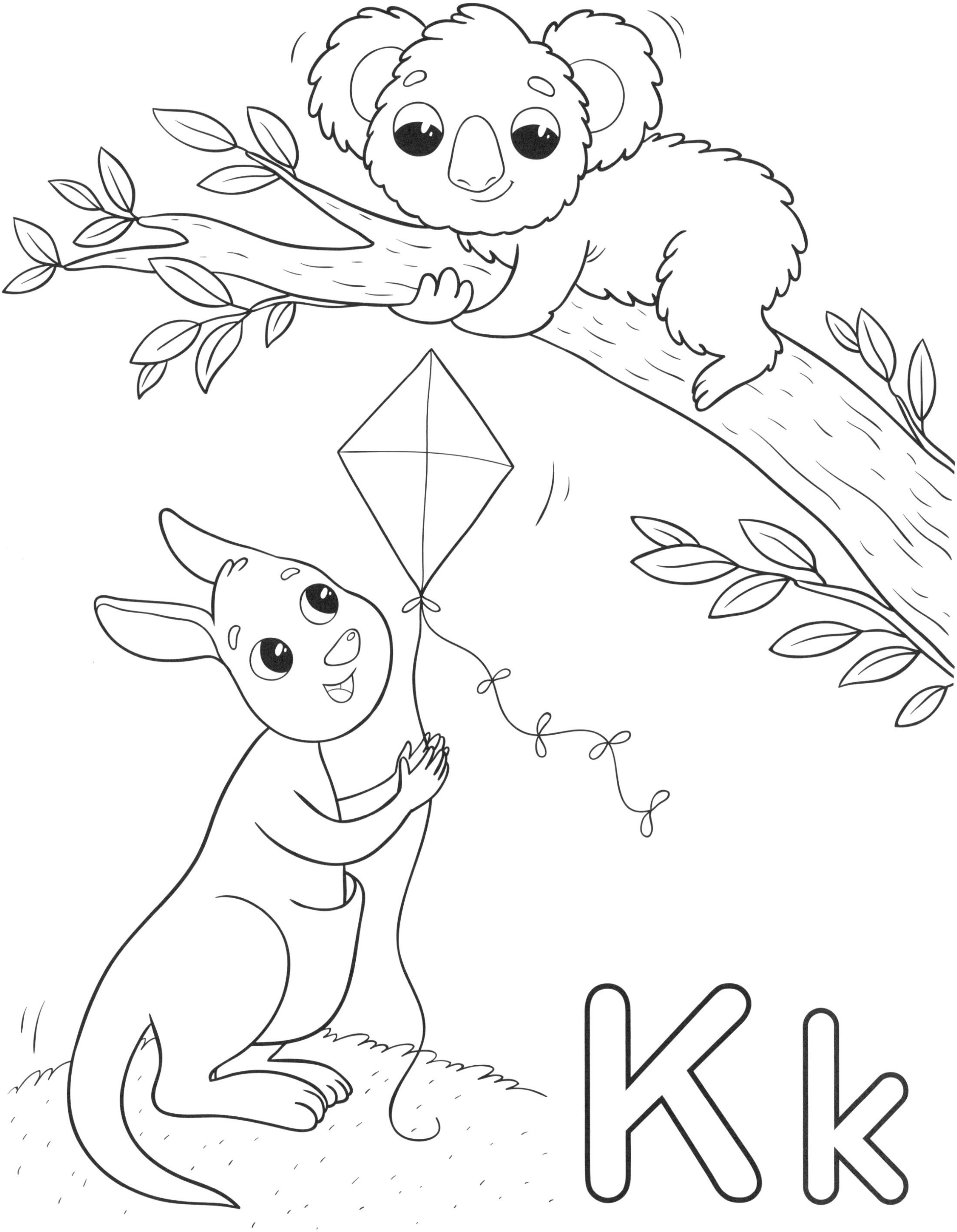
K k

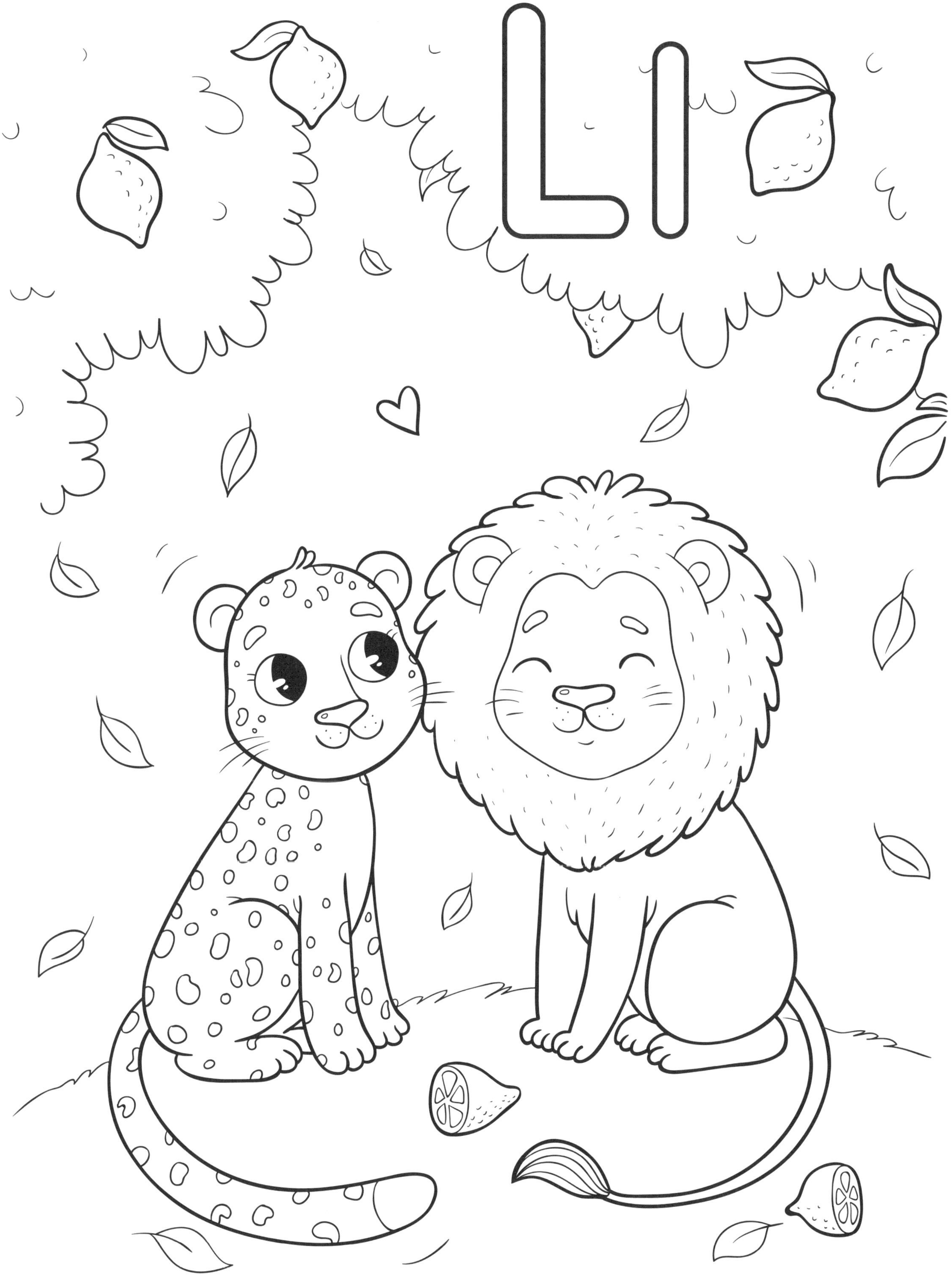
Ll

Mm

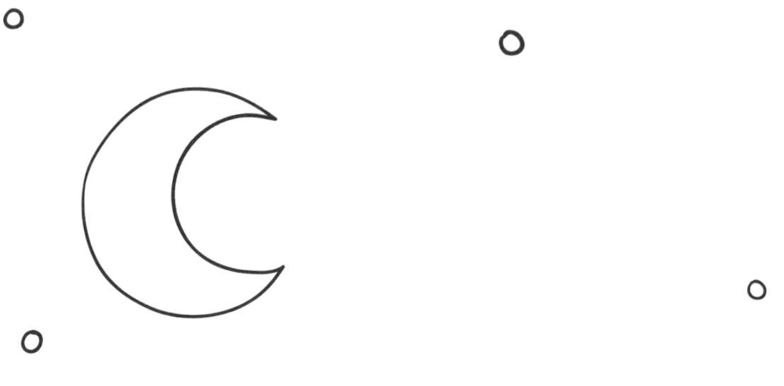

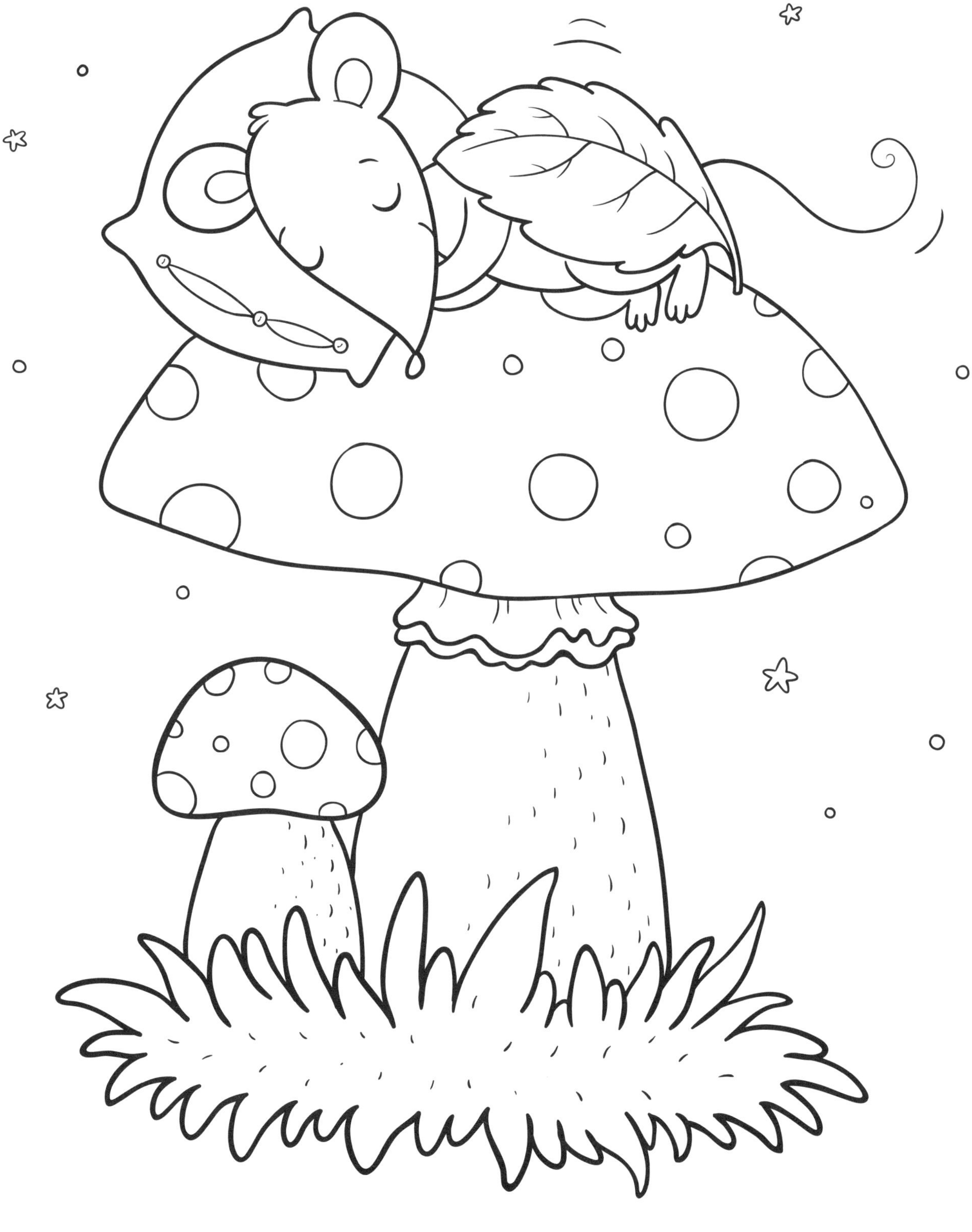

Nn

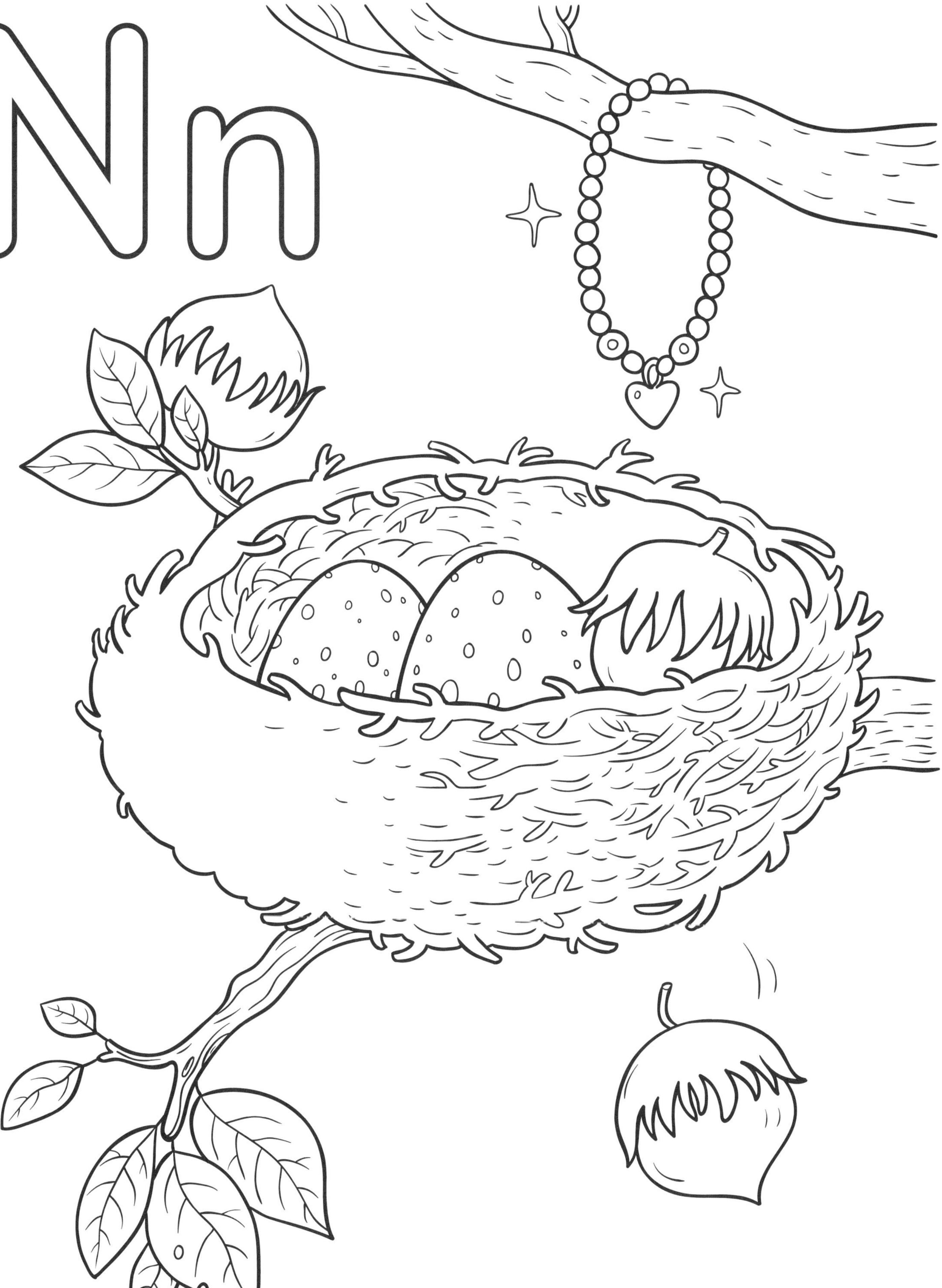

O o

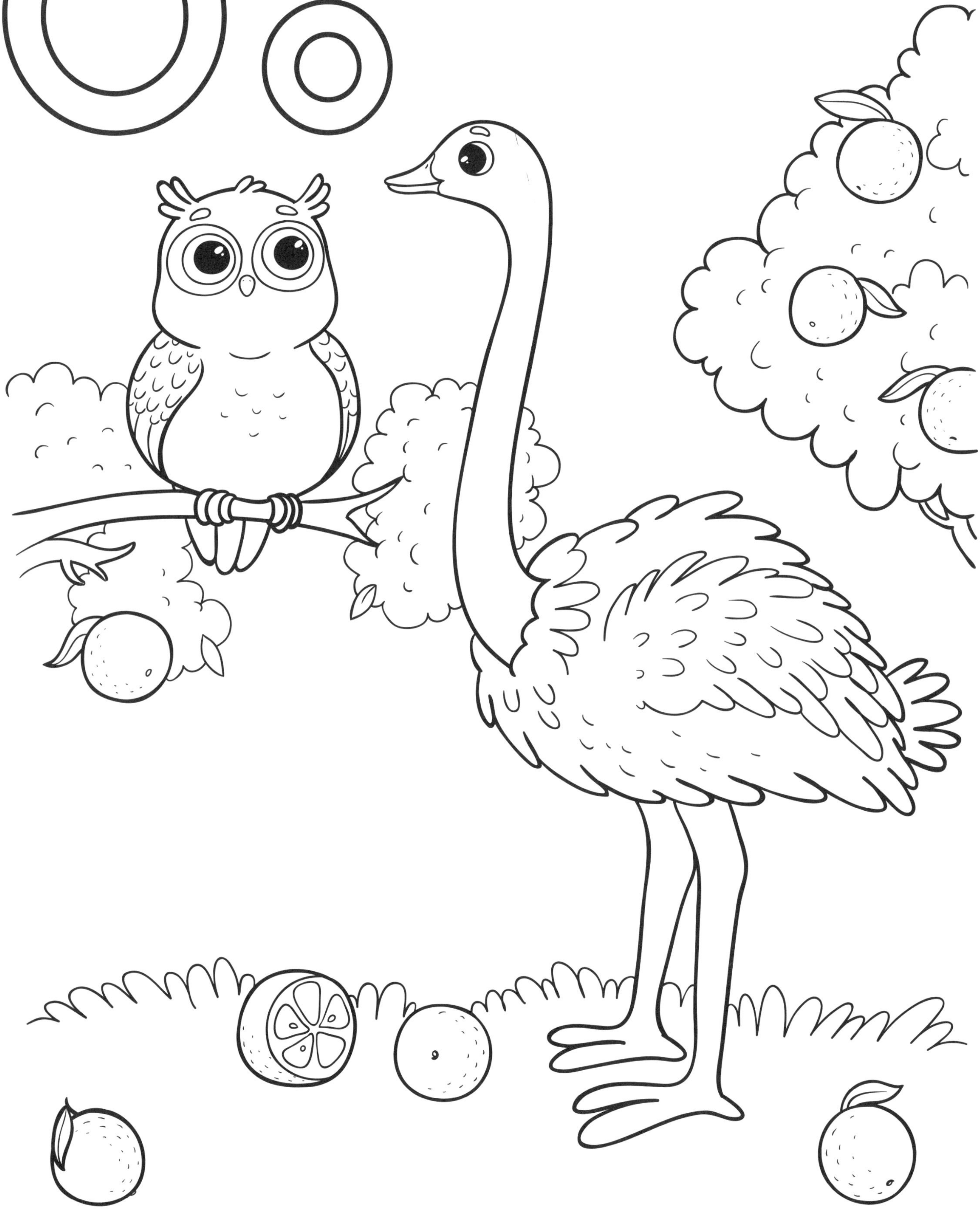

Pp

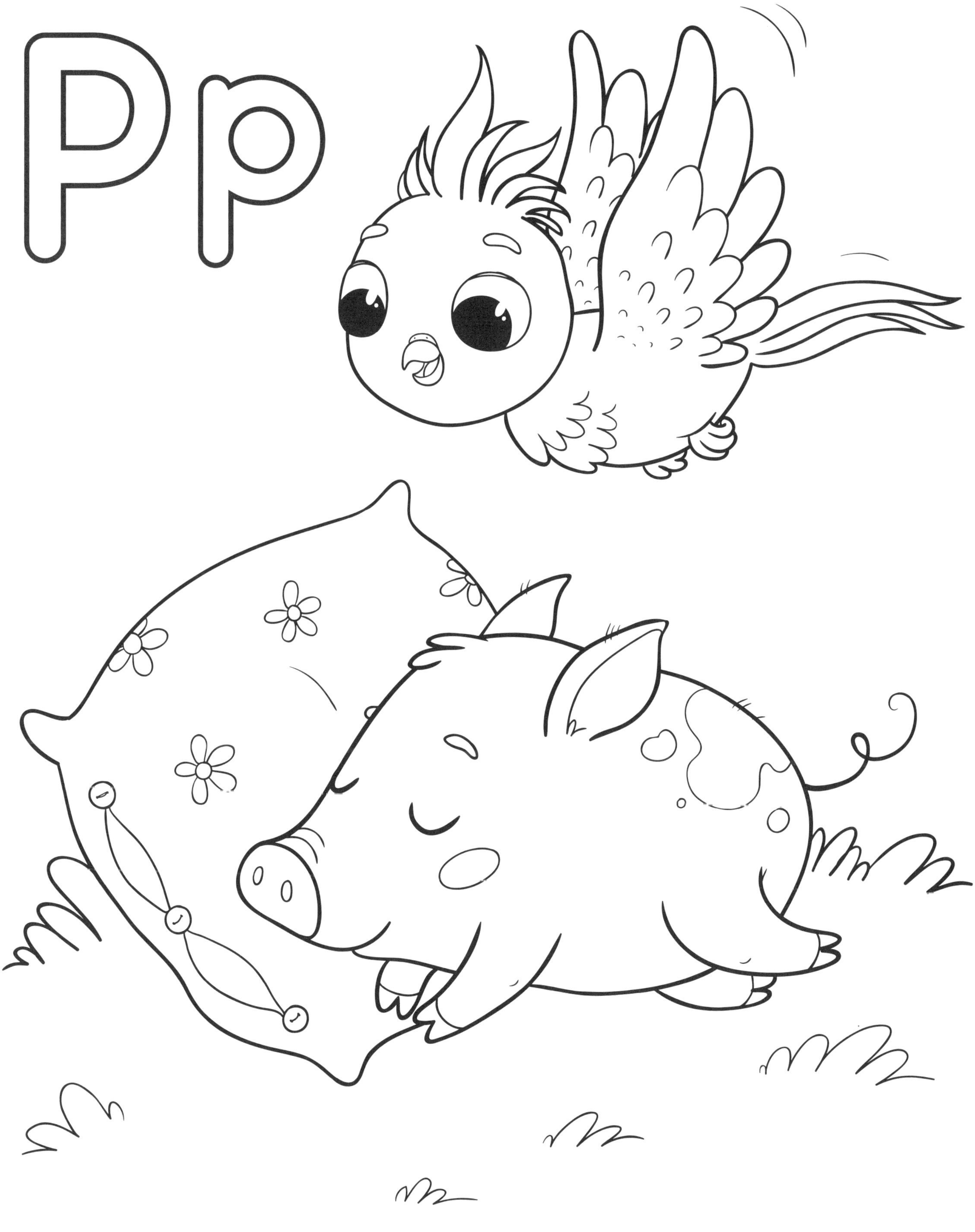

Q q

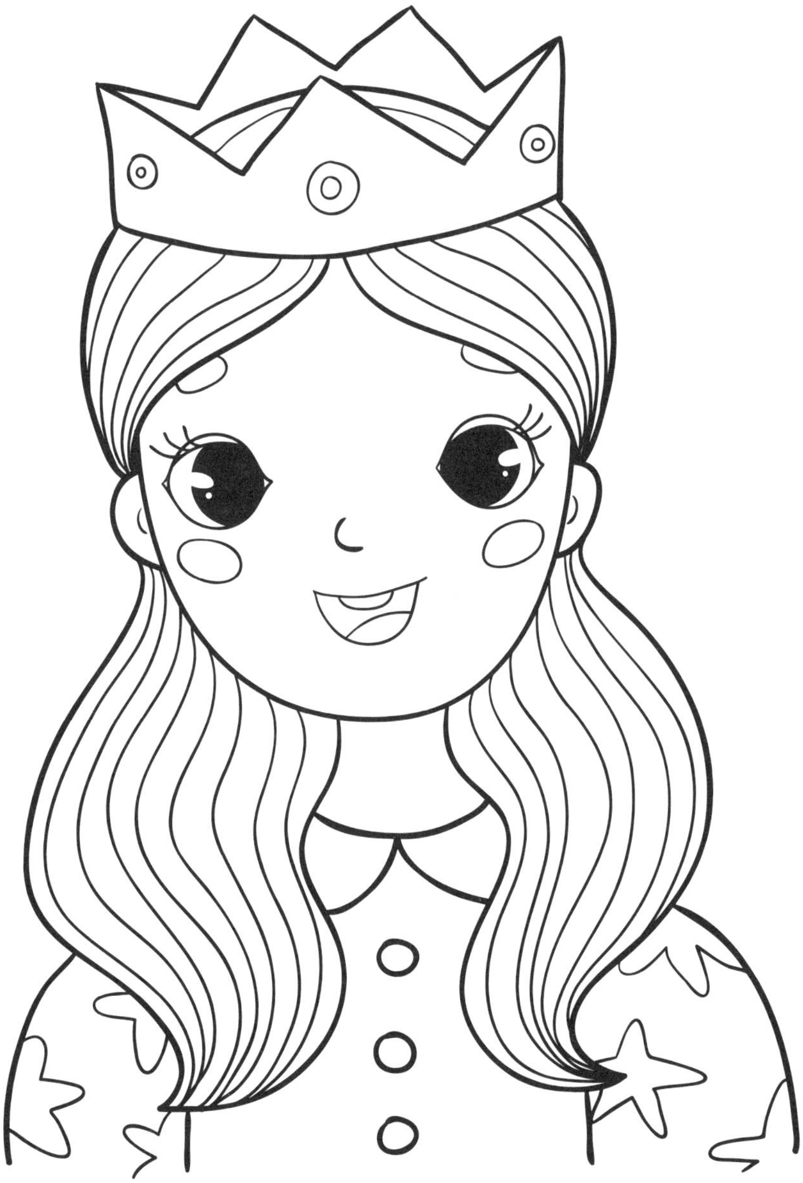

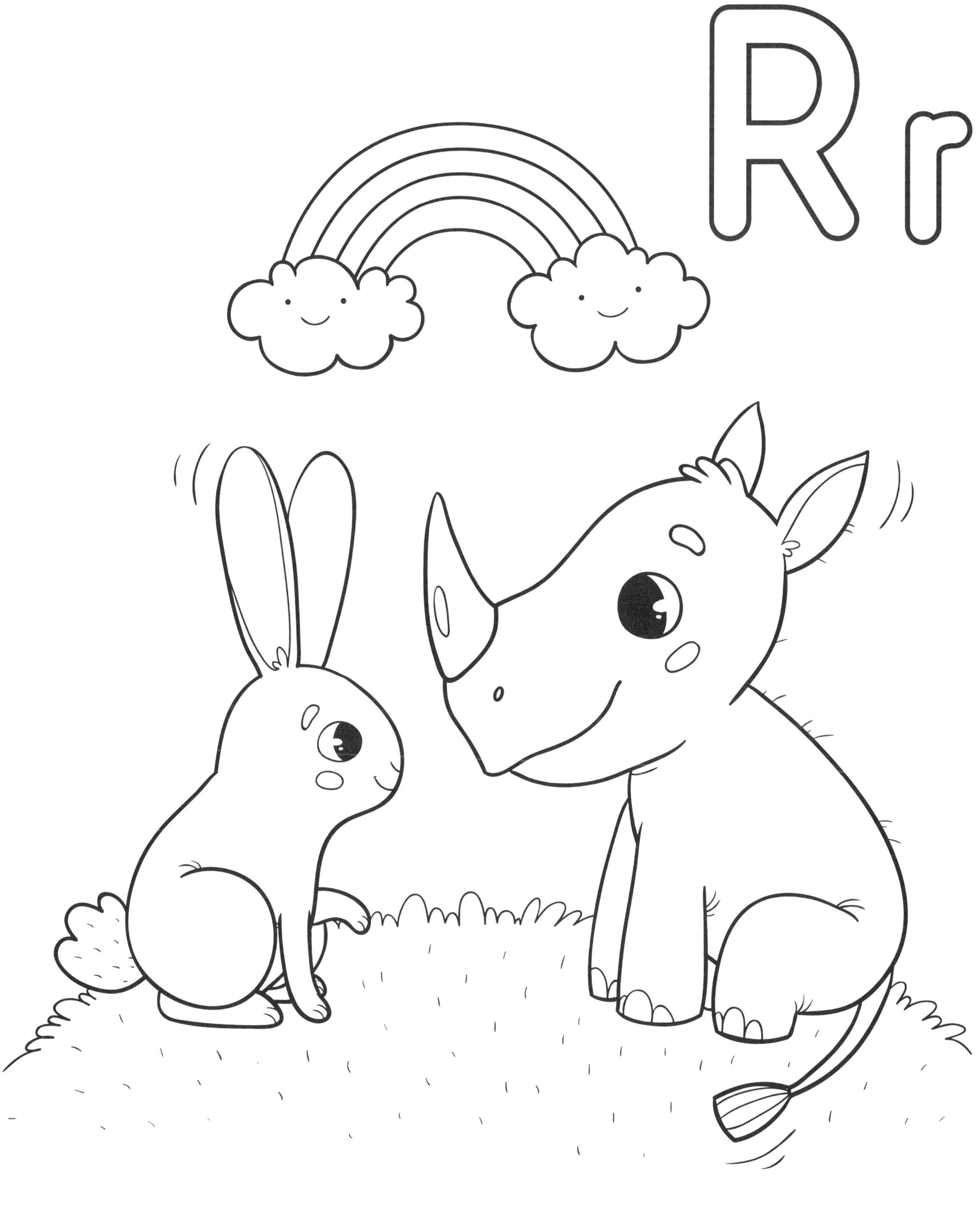
Rr

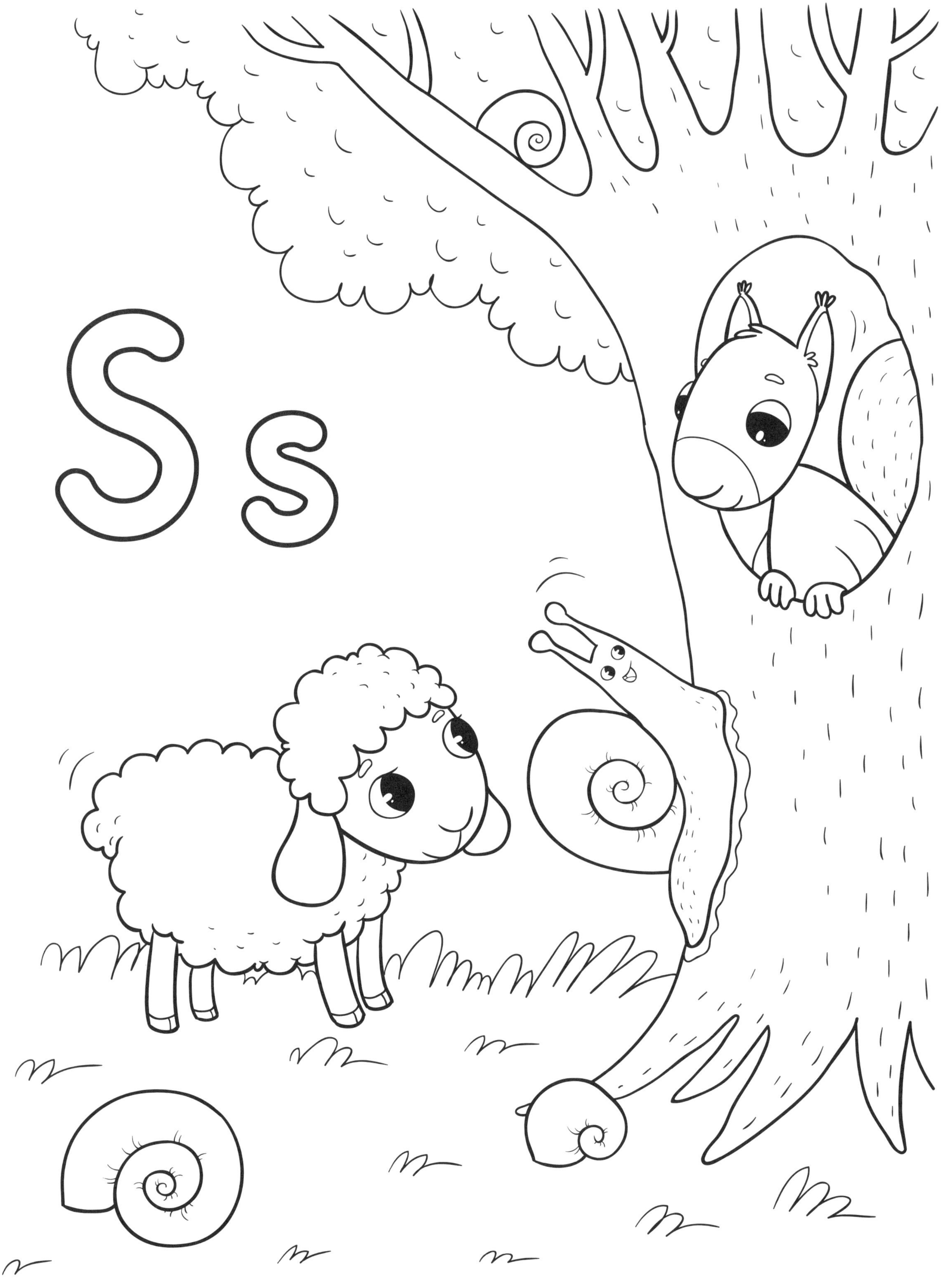
Ss

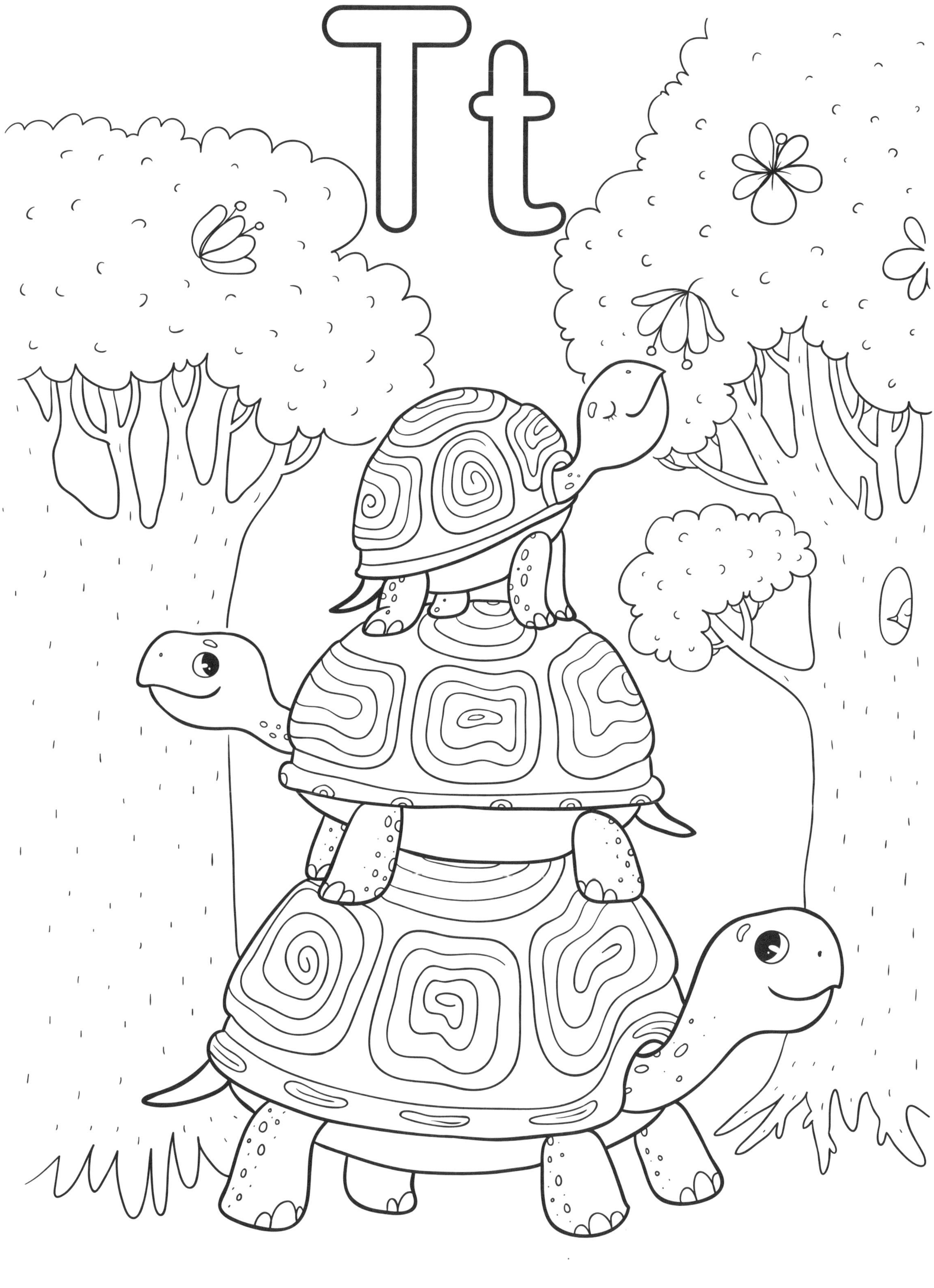
Tt

U u

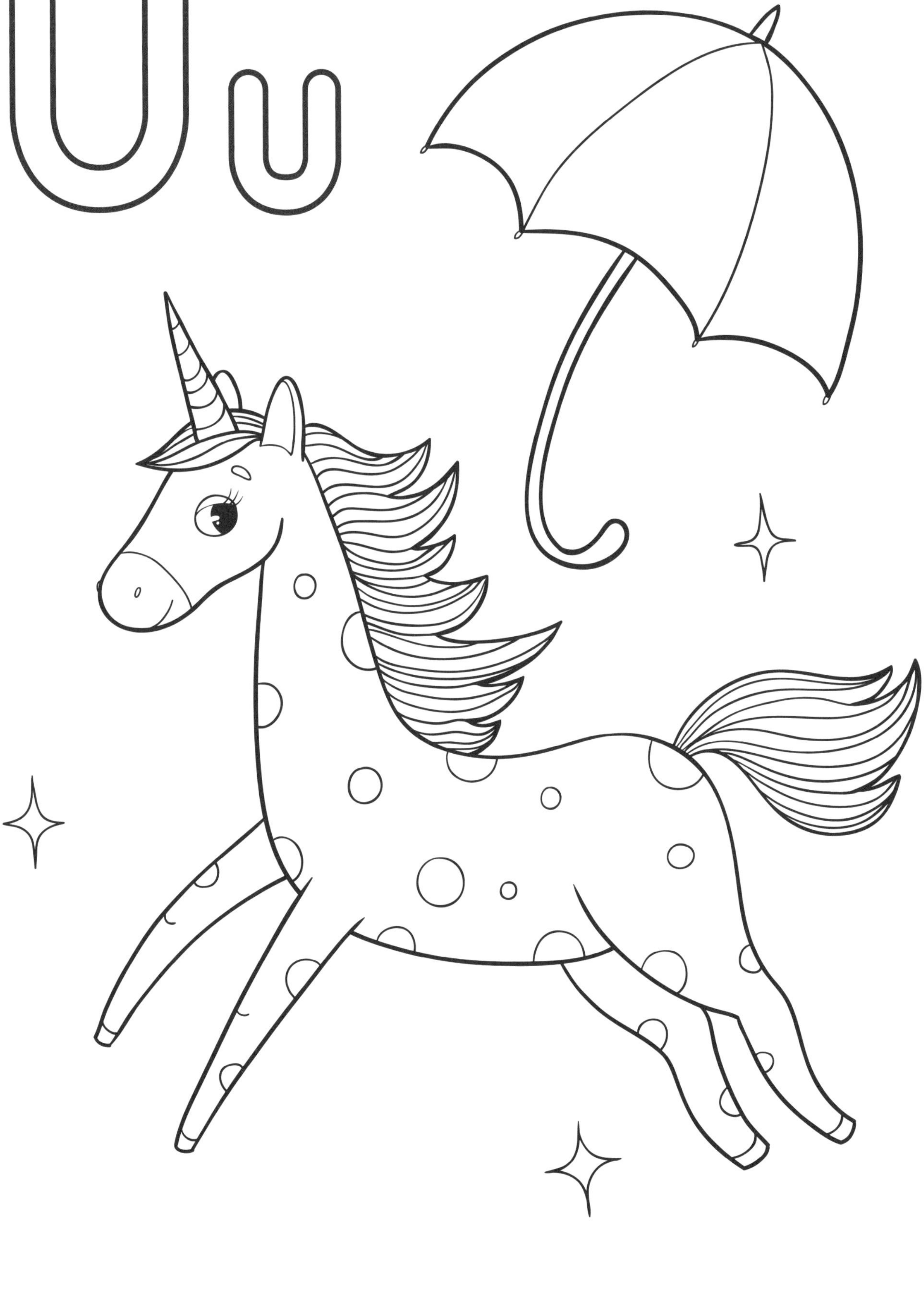

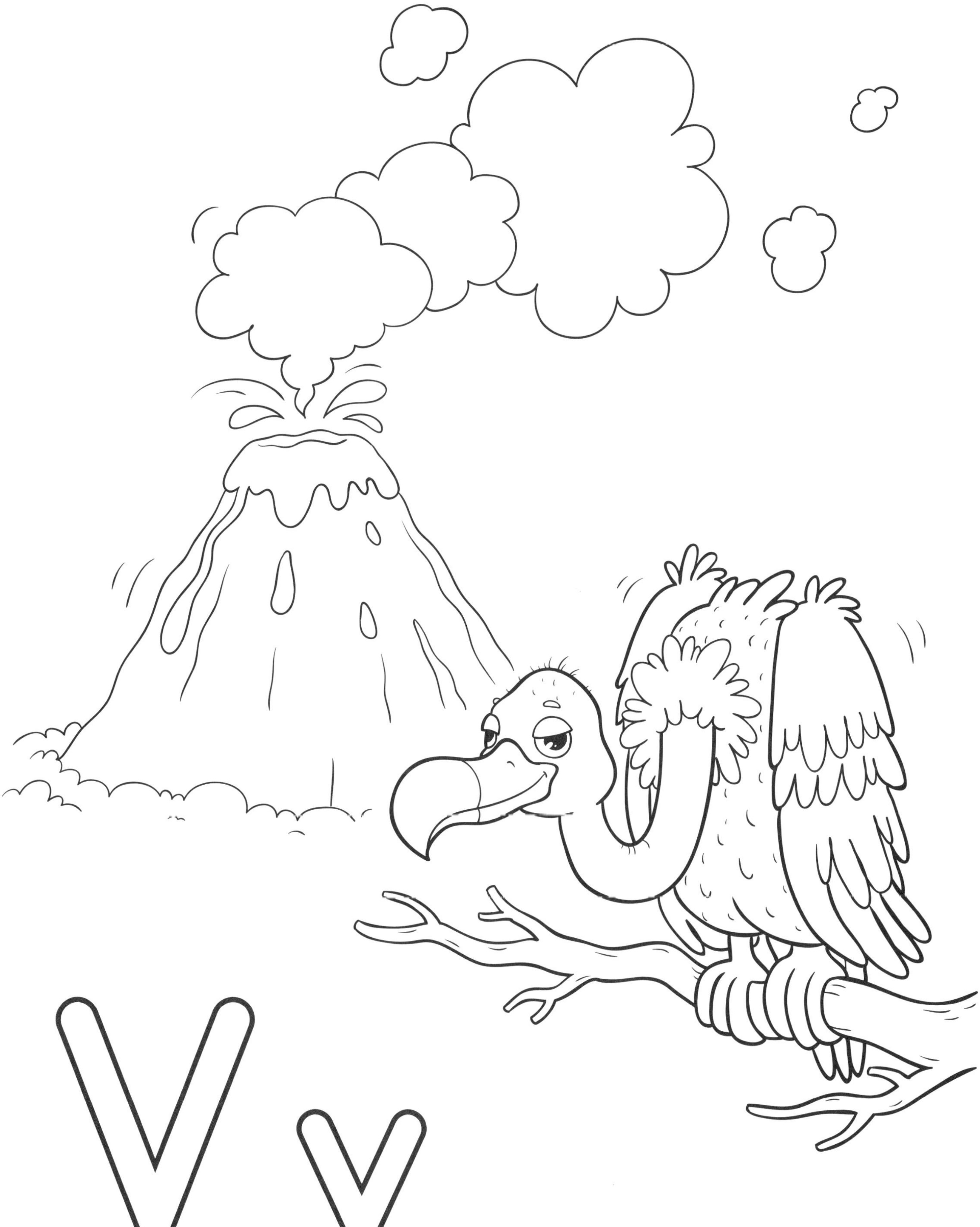
V v

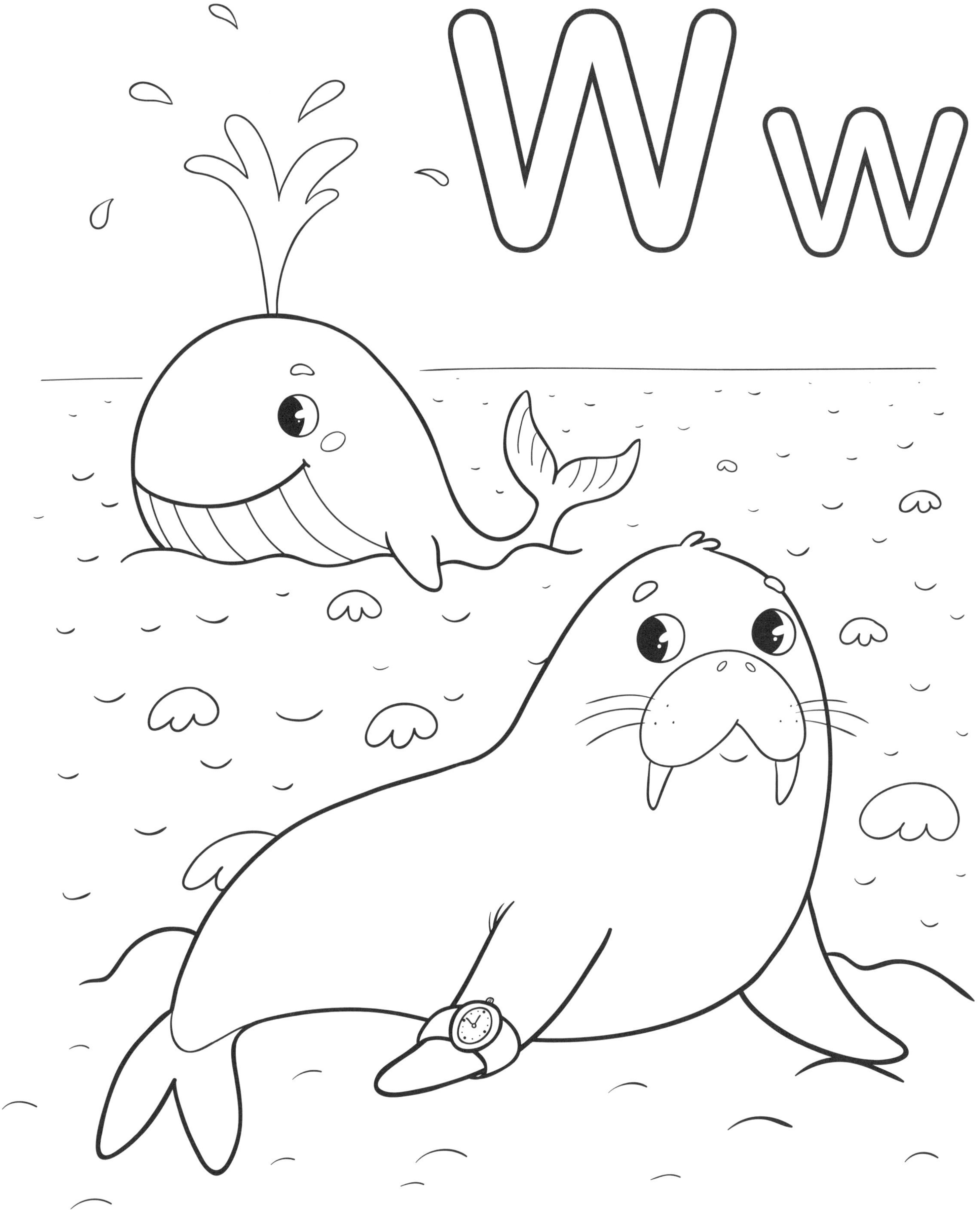
W w

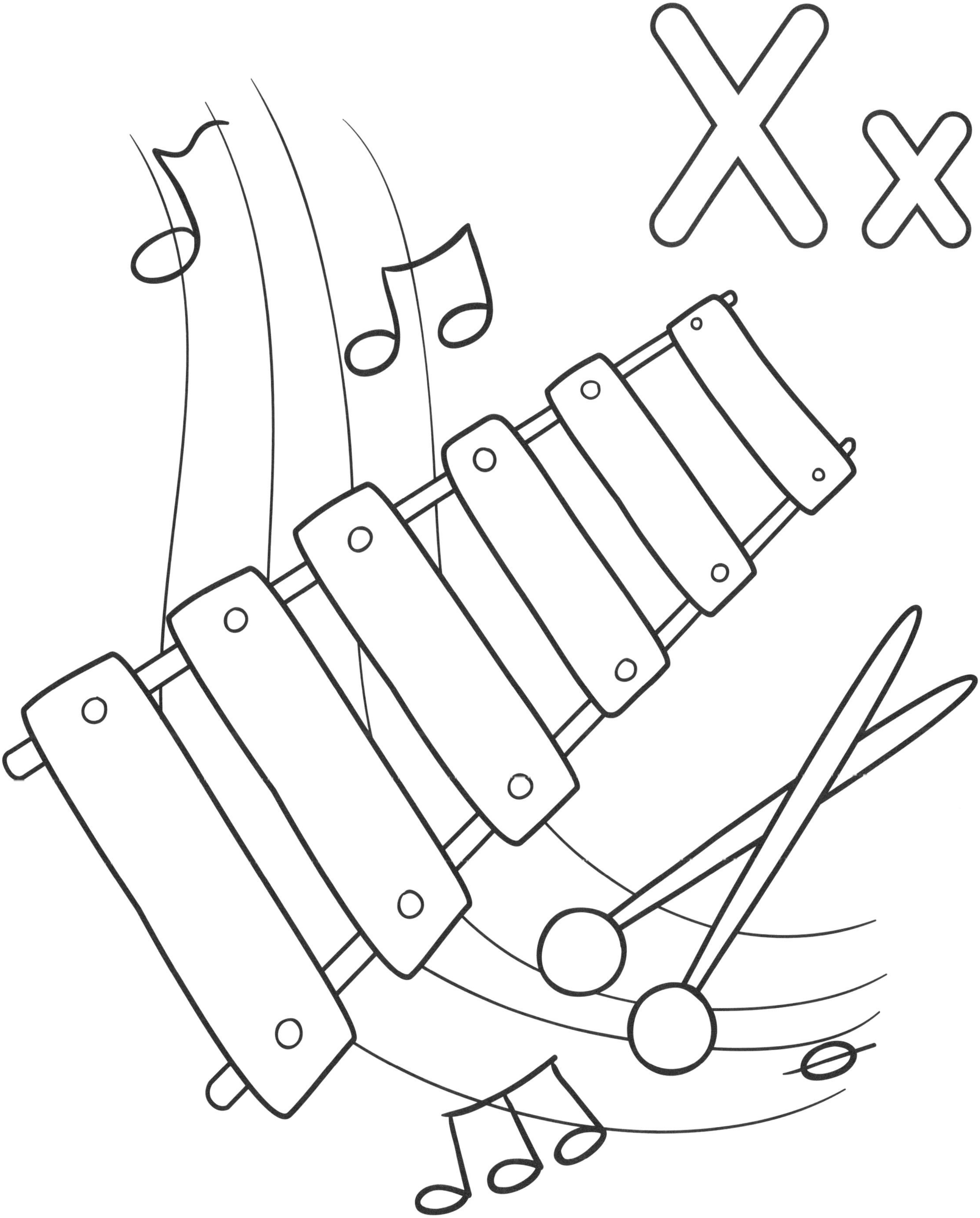
Xx

Yy

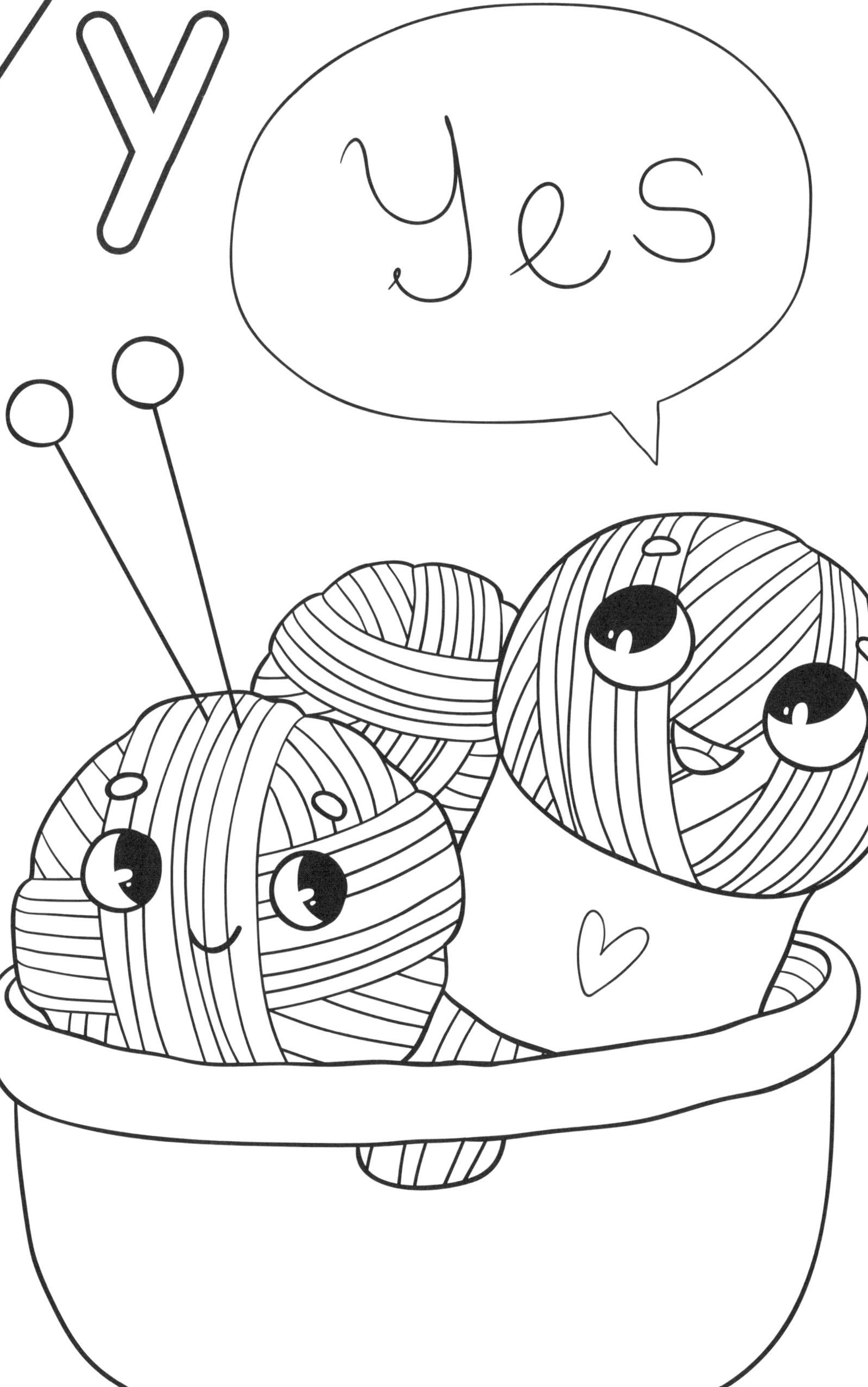

Z z

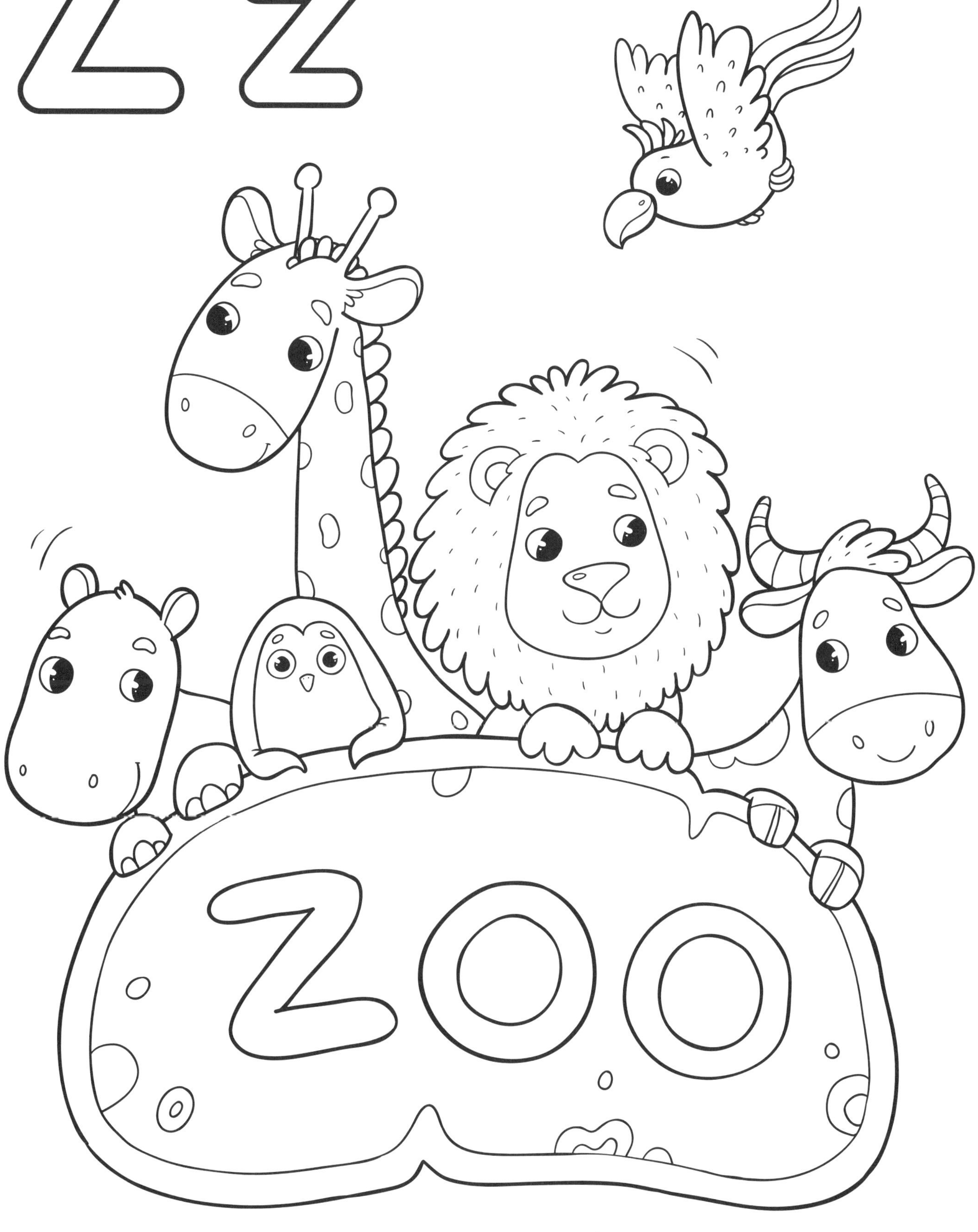

Letters

A B C D E F G

H I J K L M N O

P Q R S T U V

W X Y Z

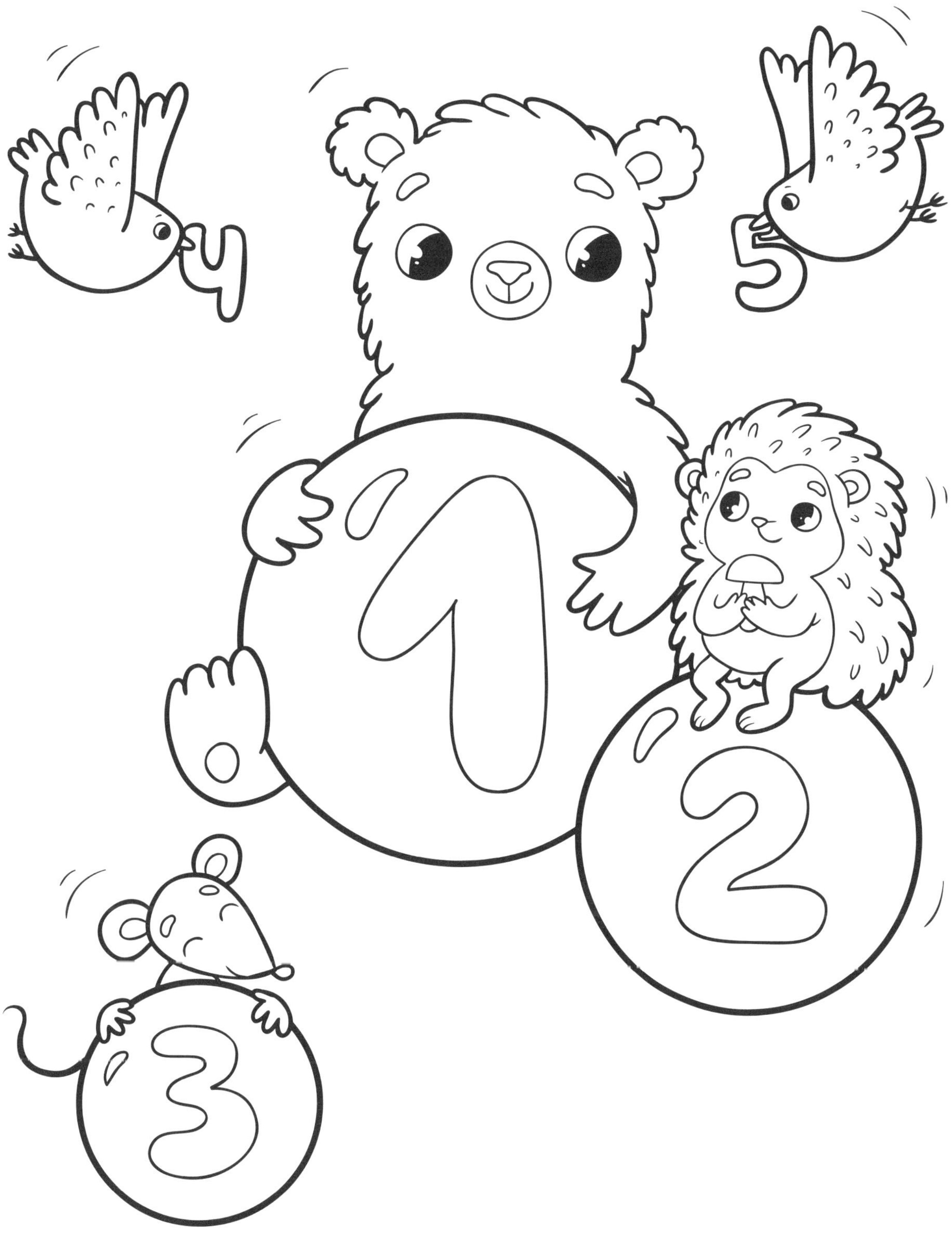

Numbers

0

Zero

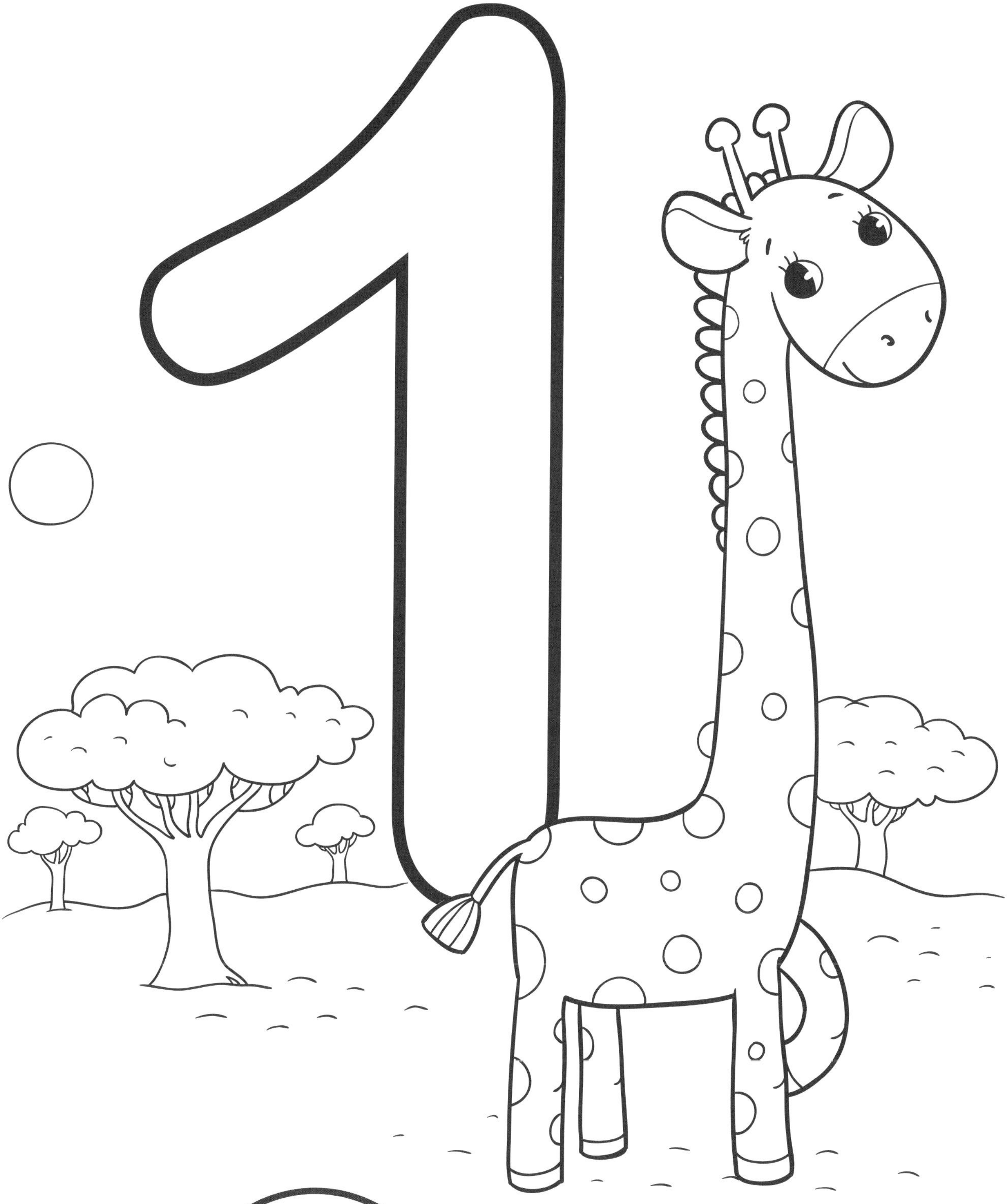

One

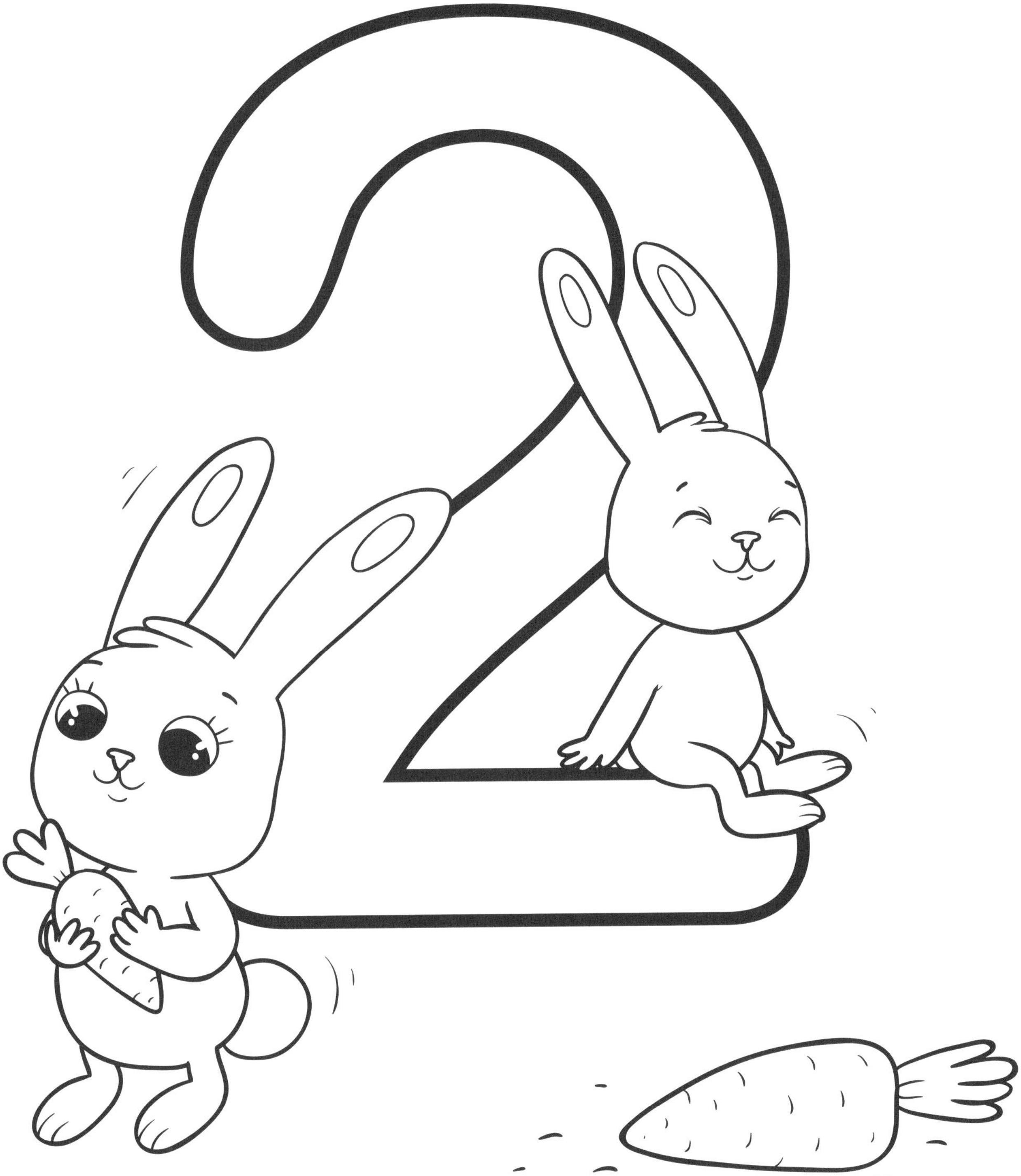

Two

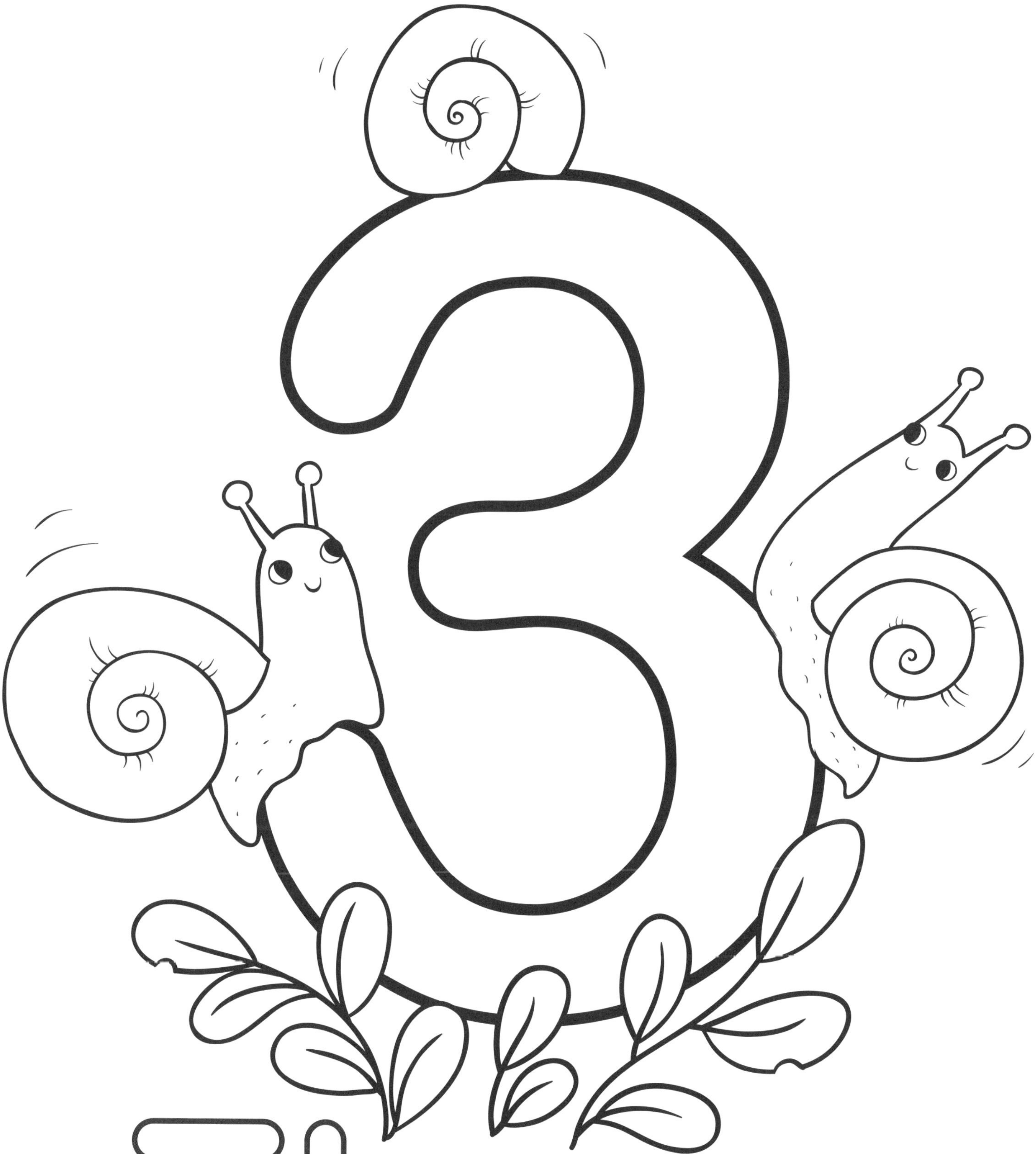

Three

Four

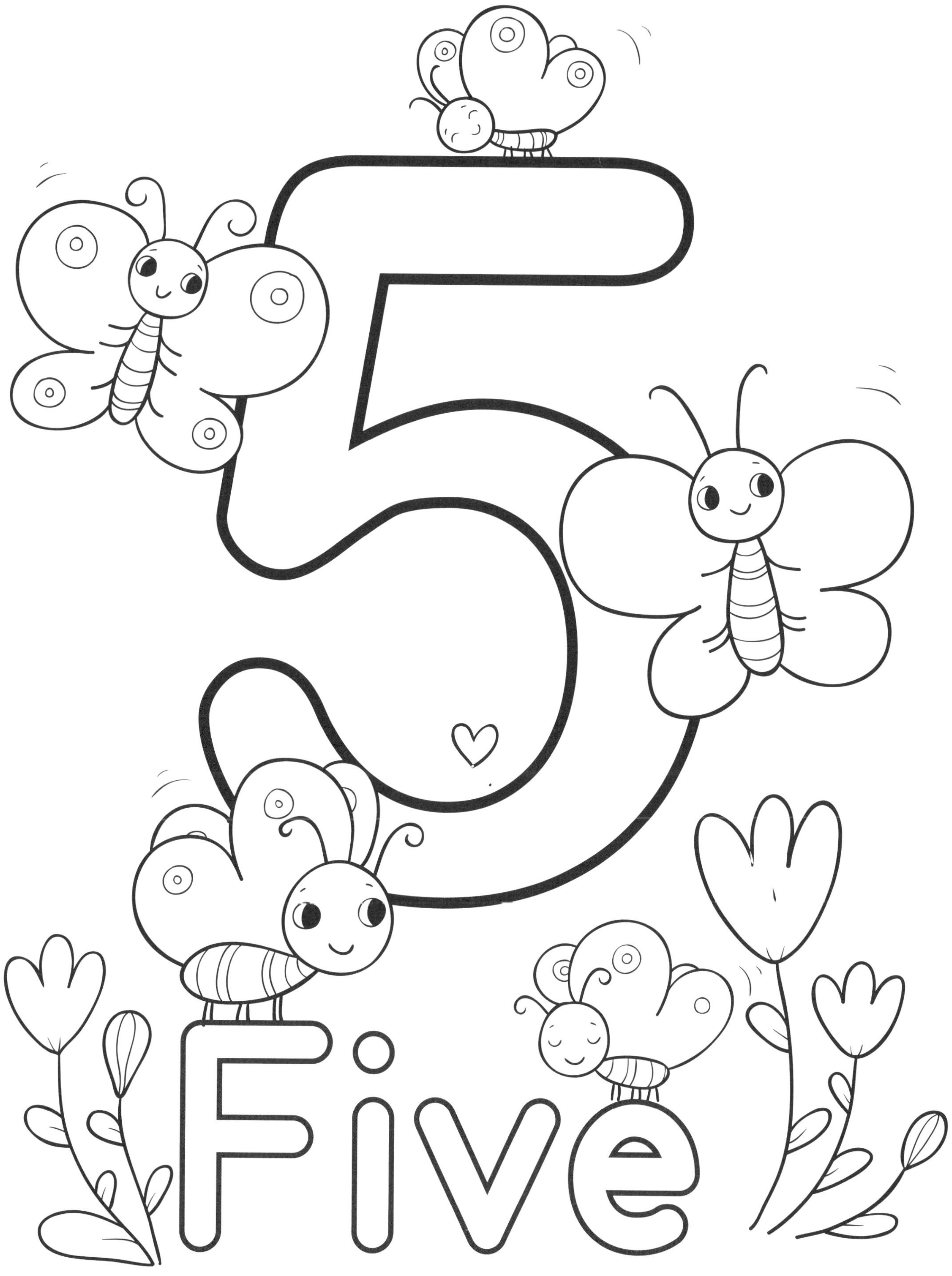
5
Five

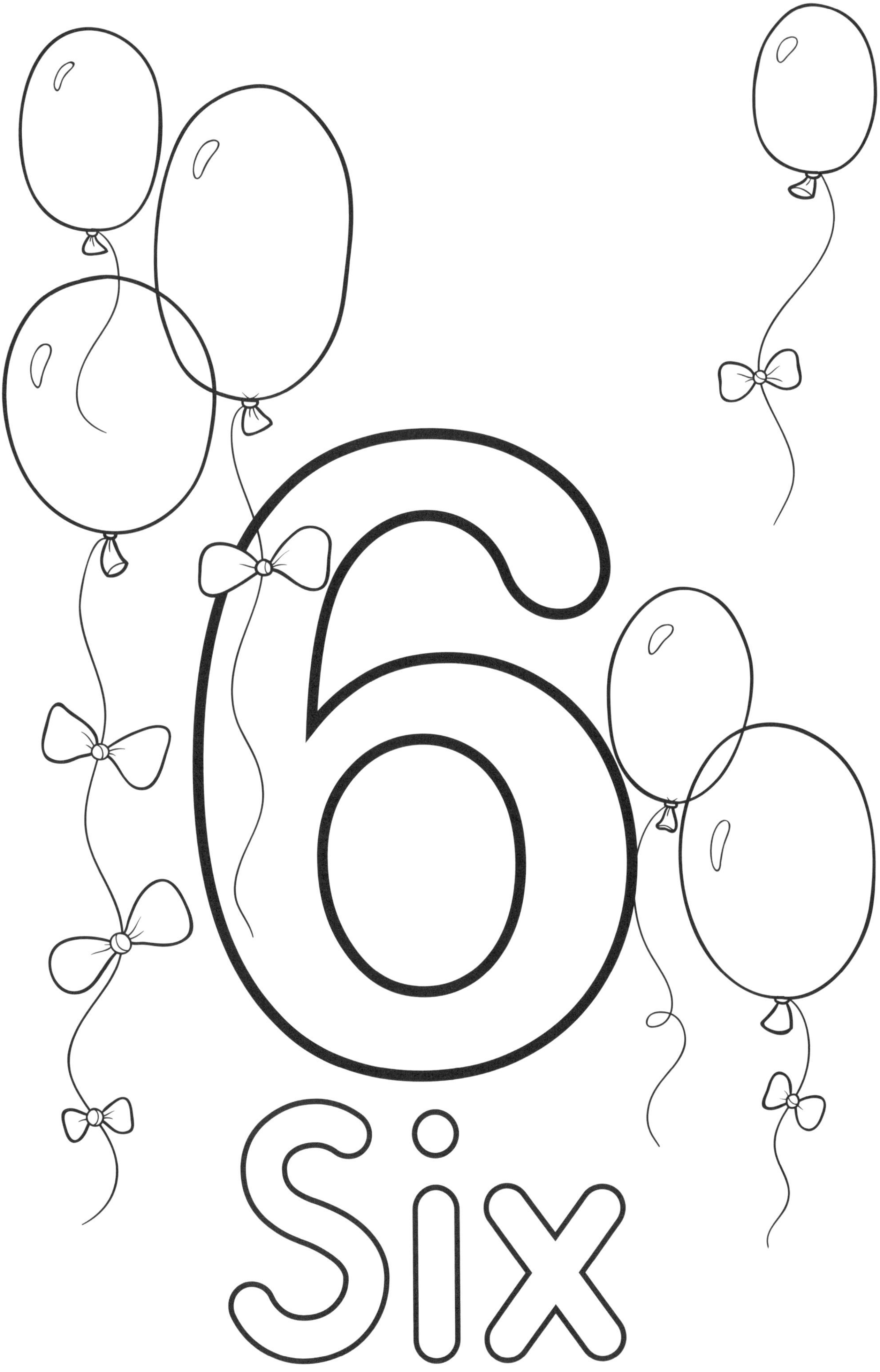
6
Six

7
Seven

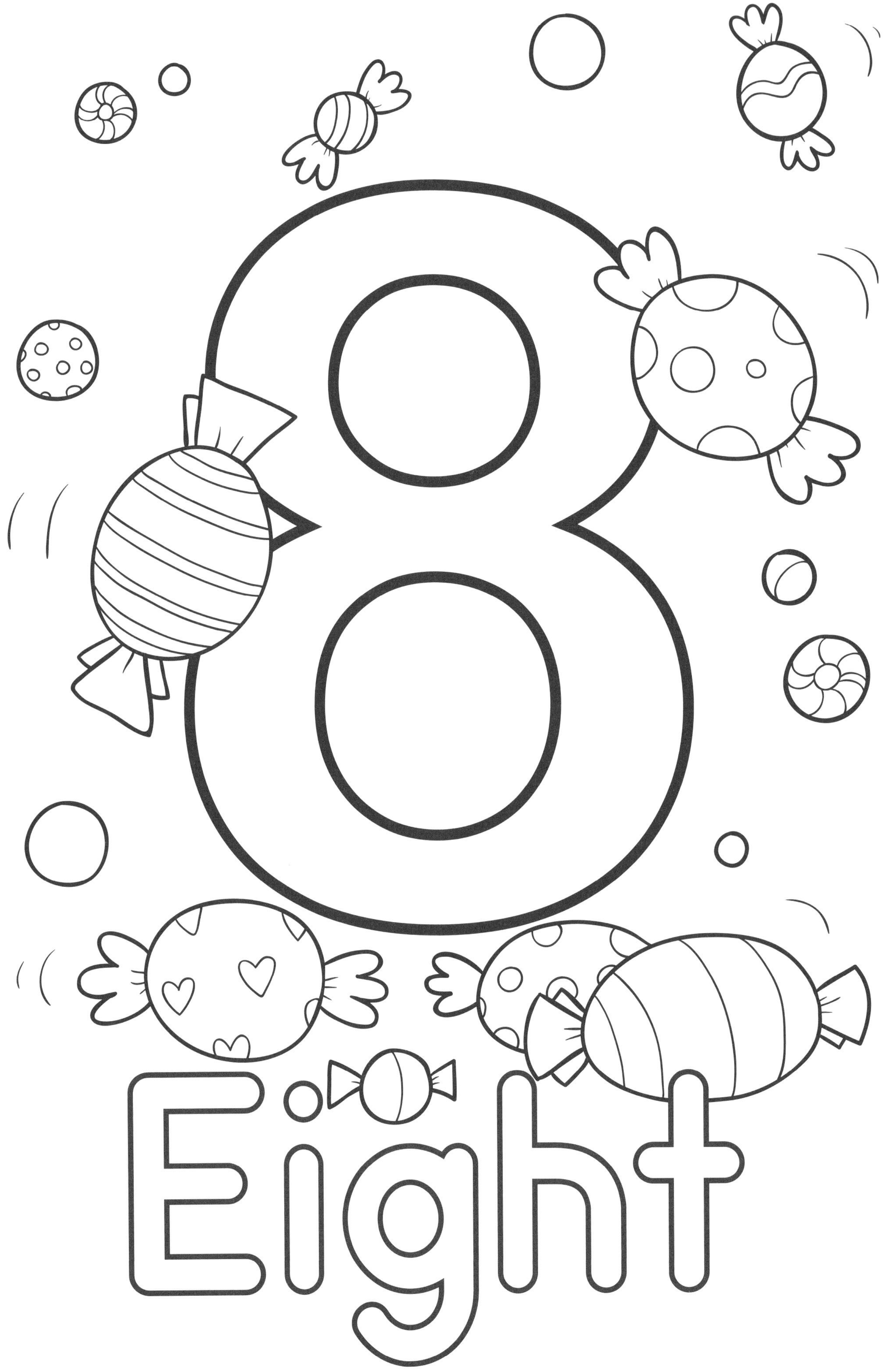
8
Eight

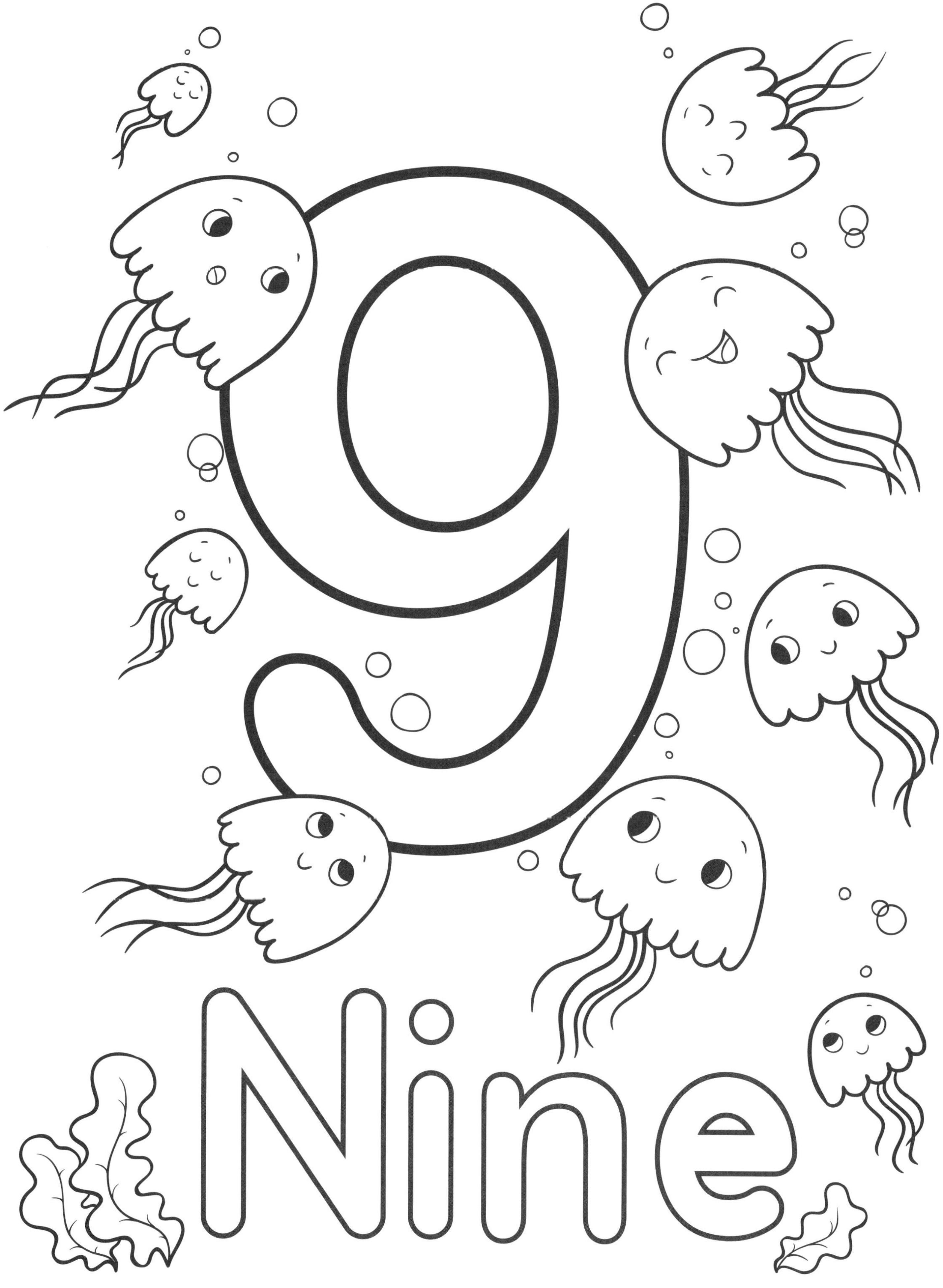
9
Nine

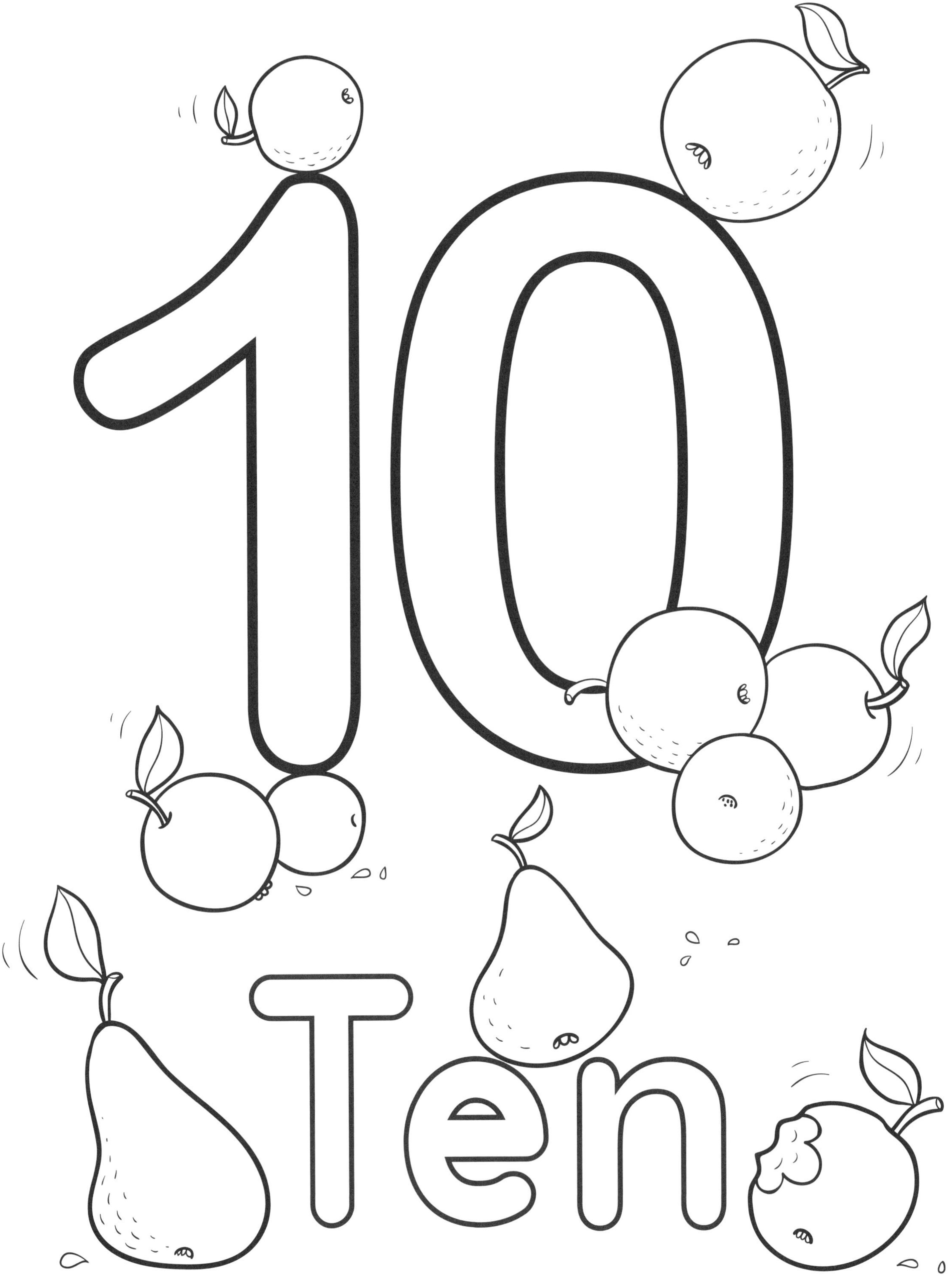
10
Ten

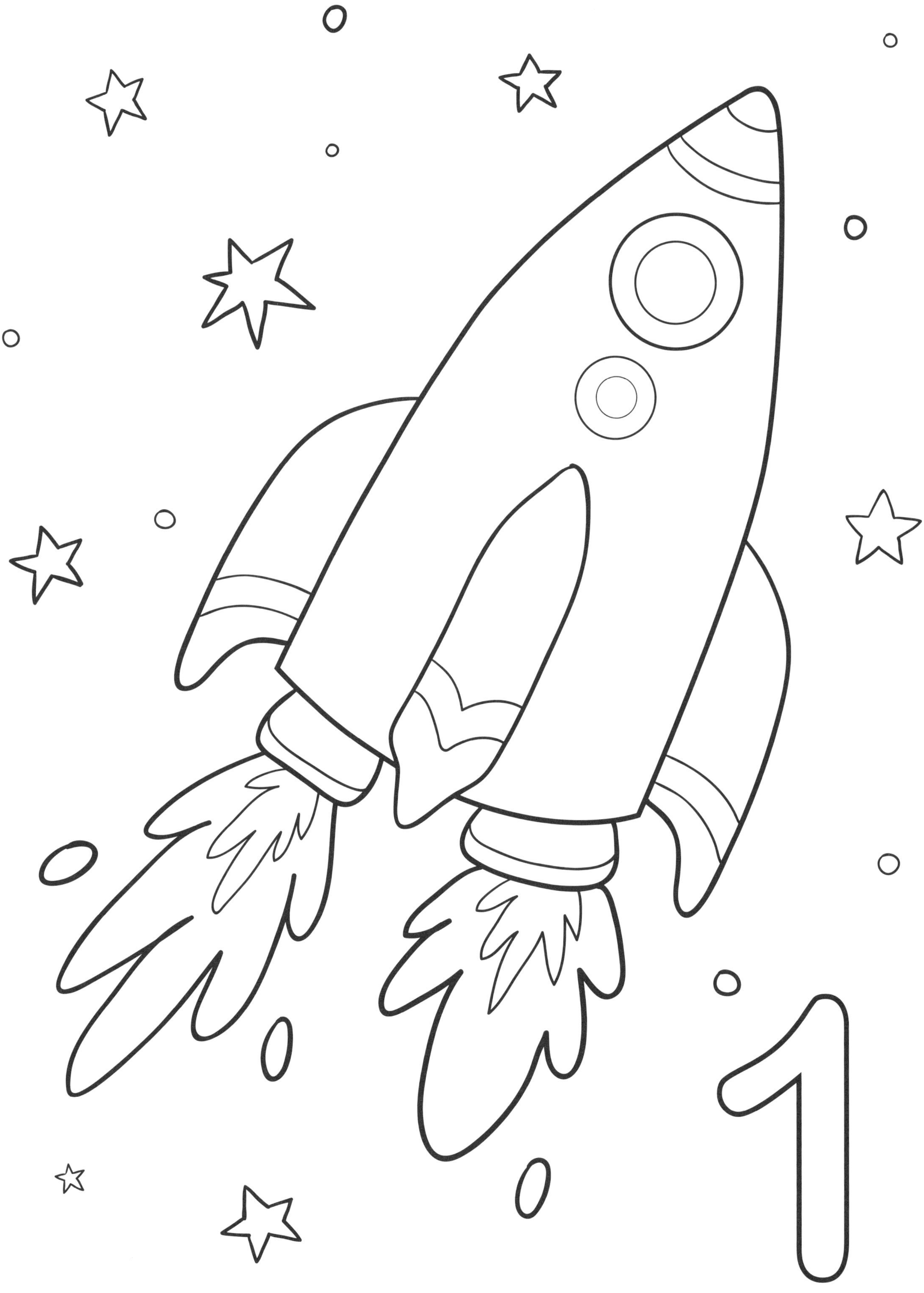
1

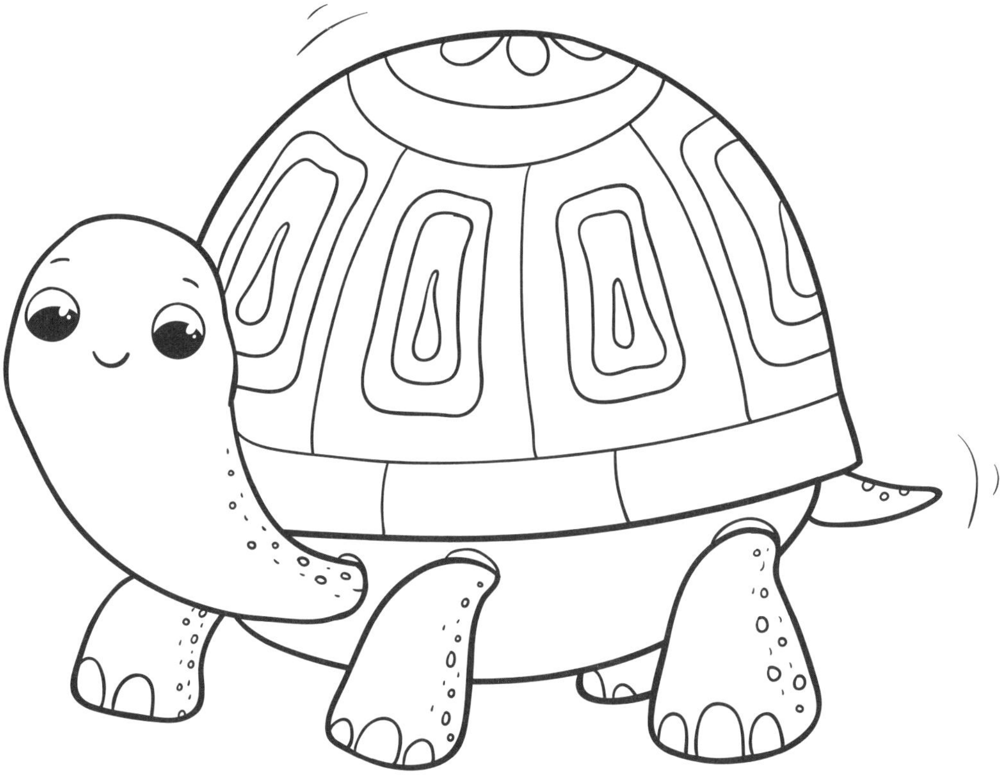

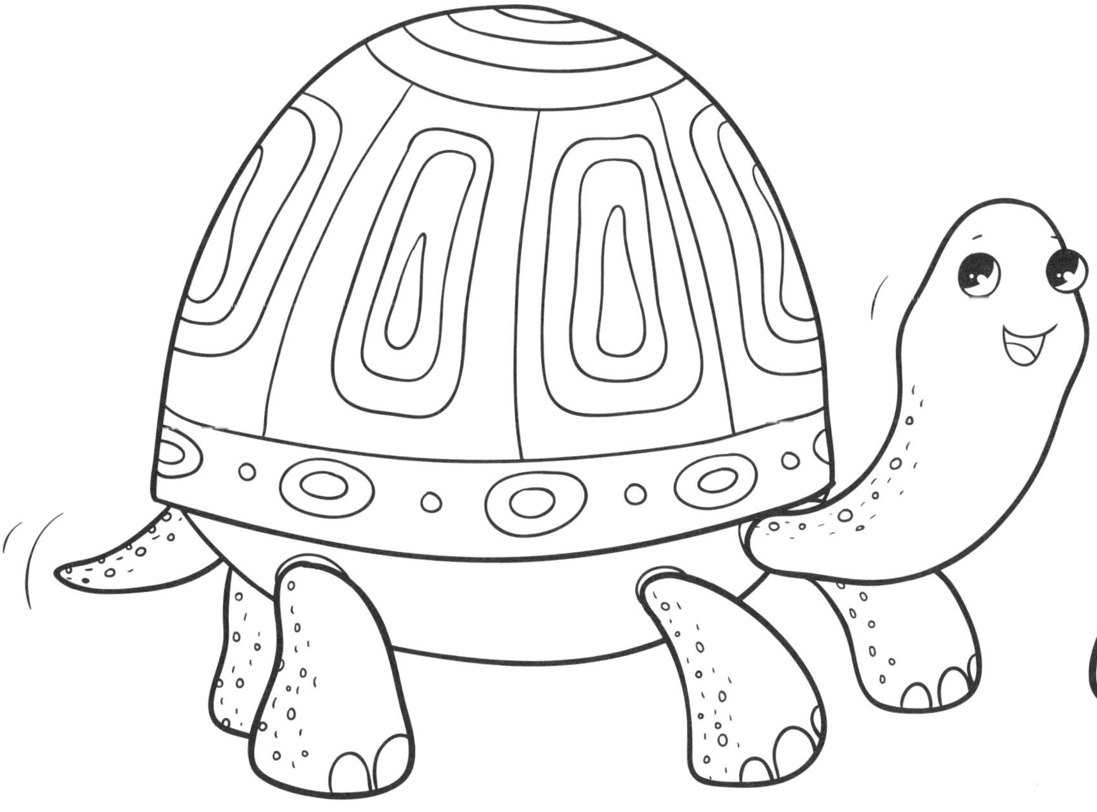

2

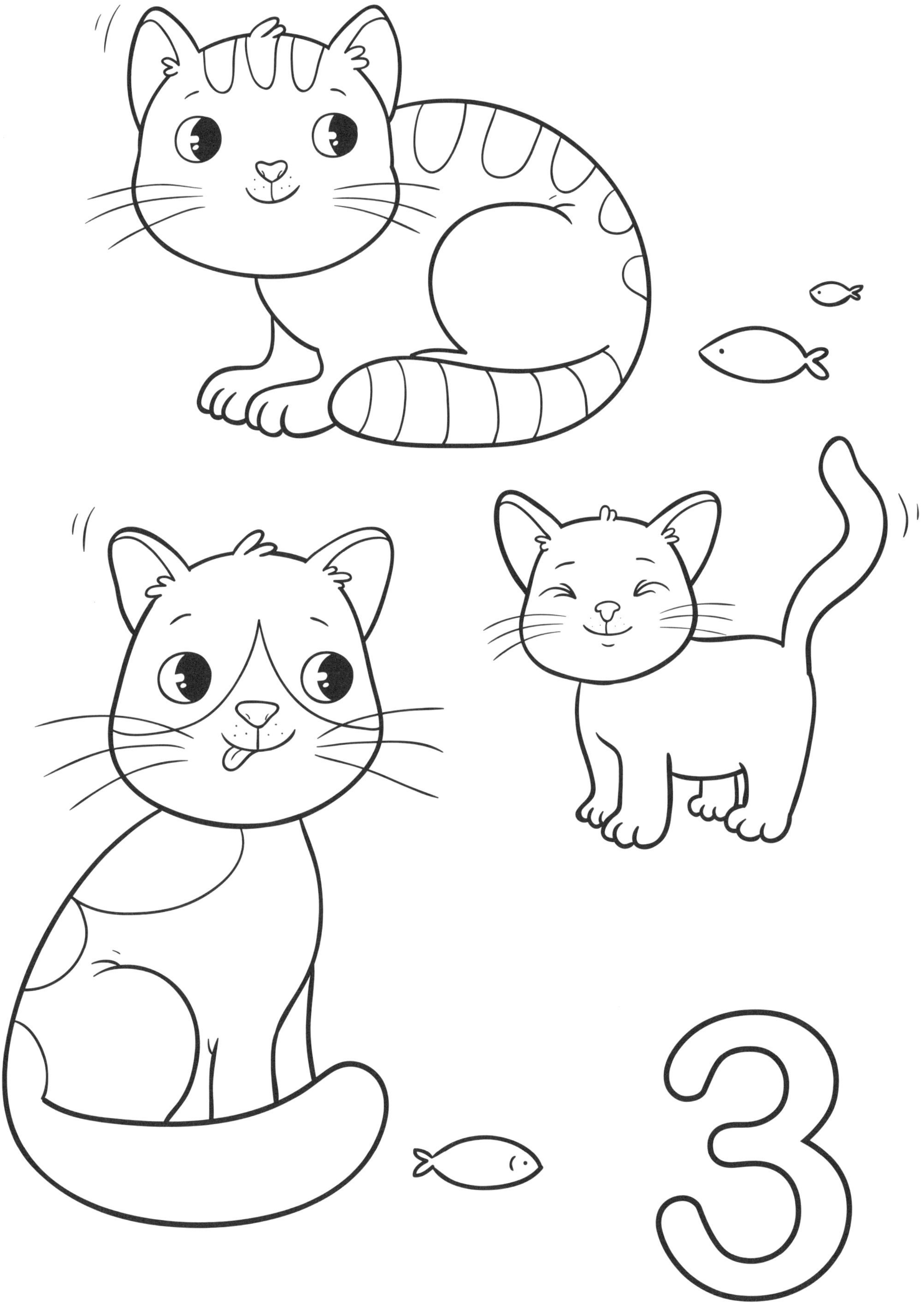
3

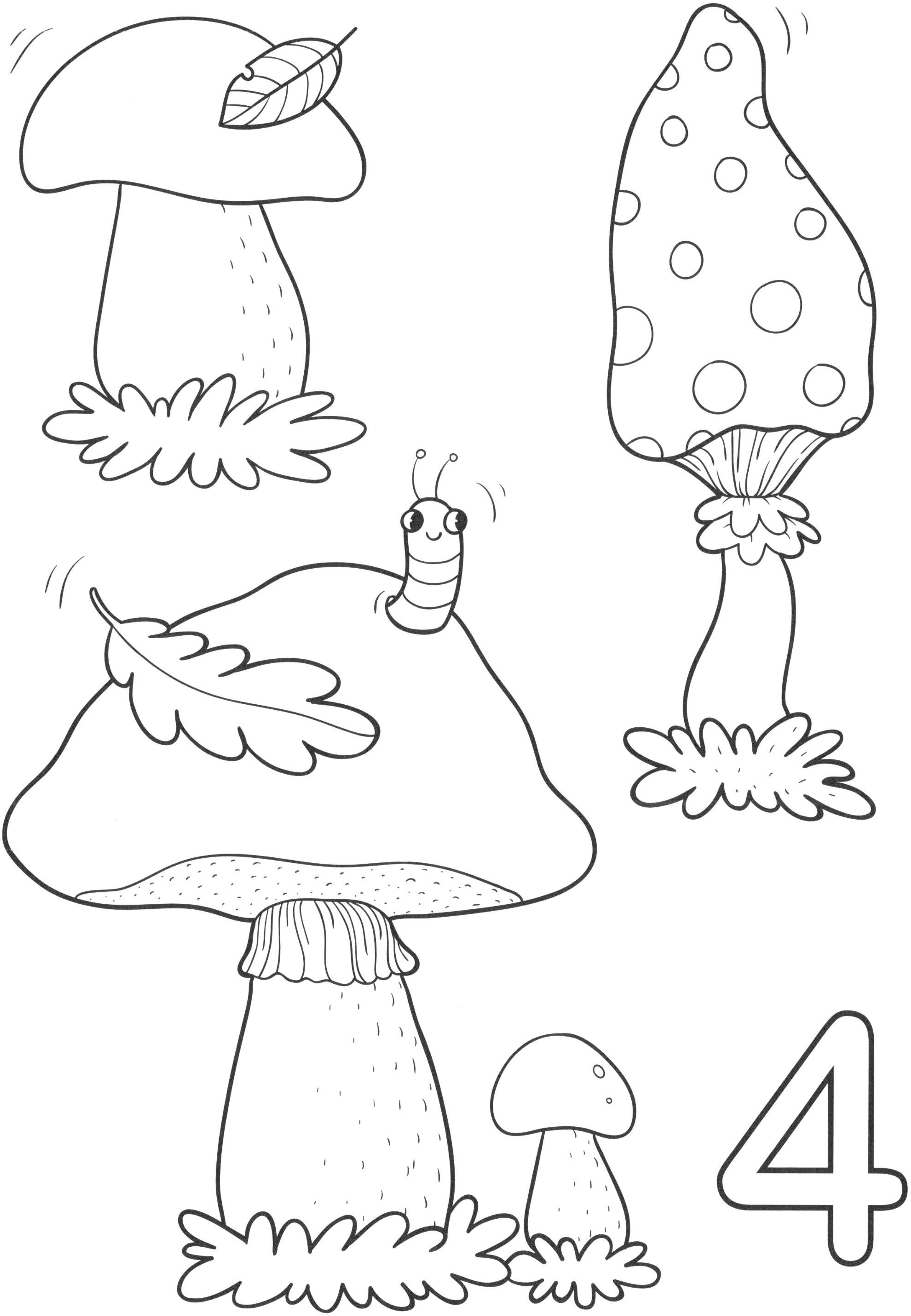
4

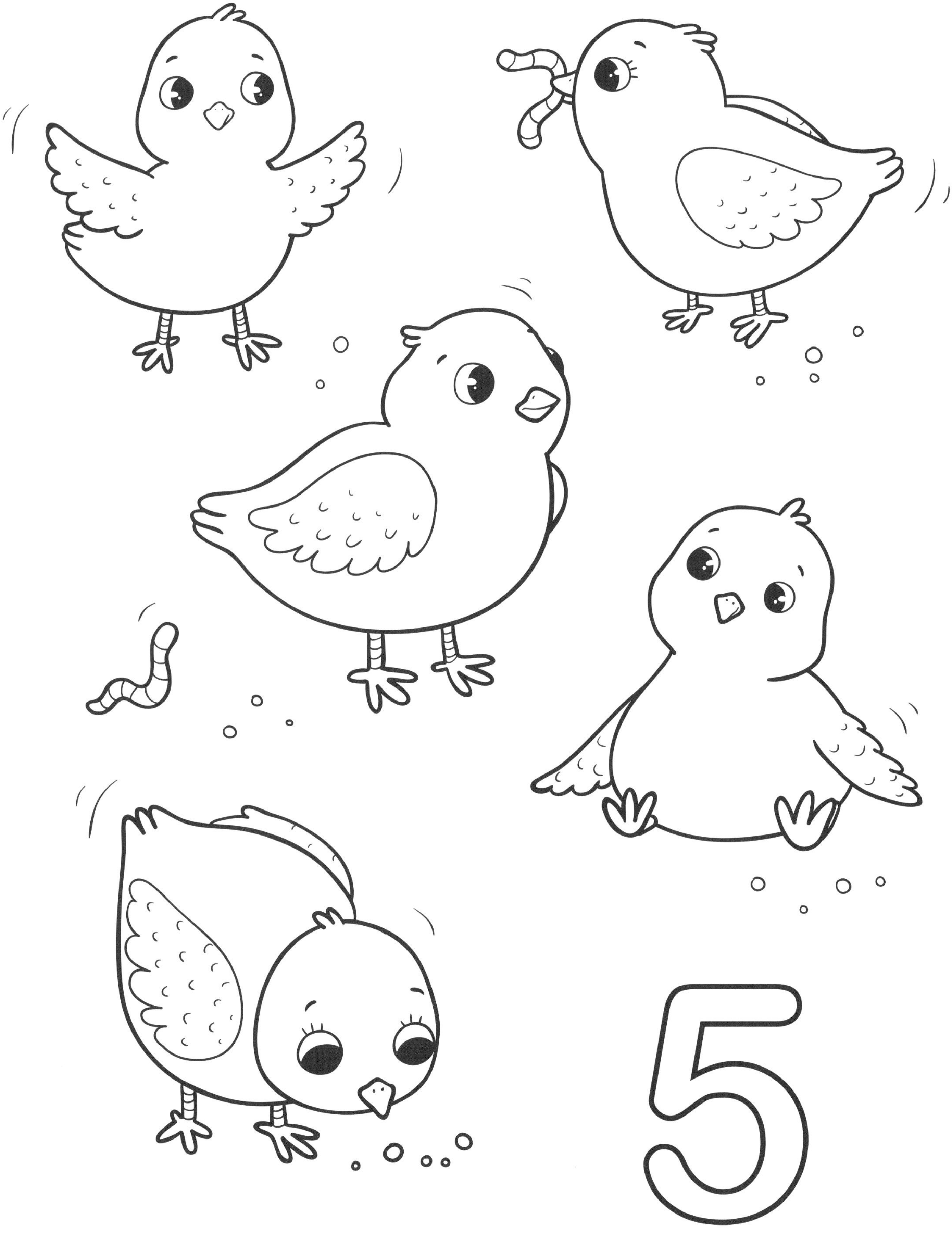
5

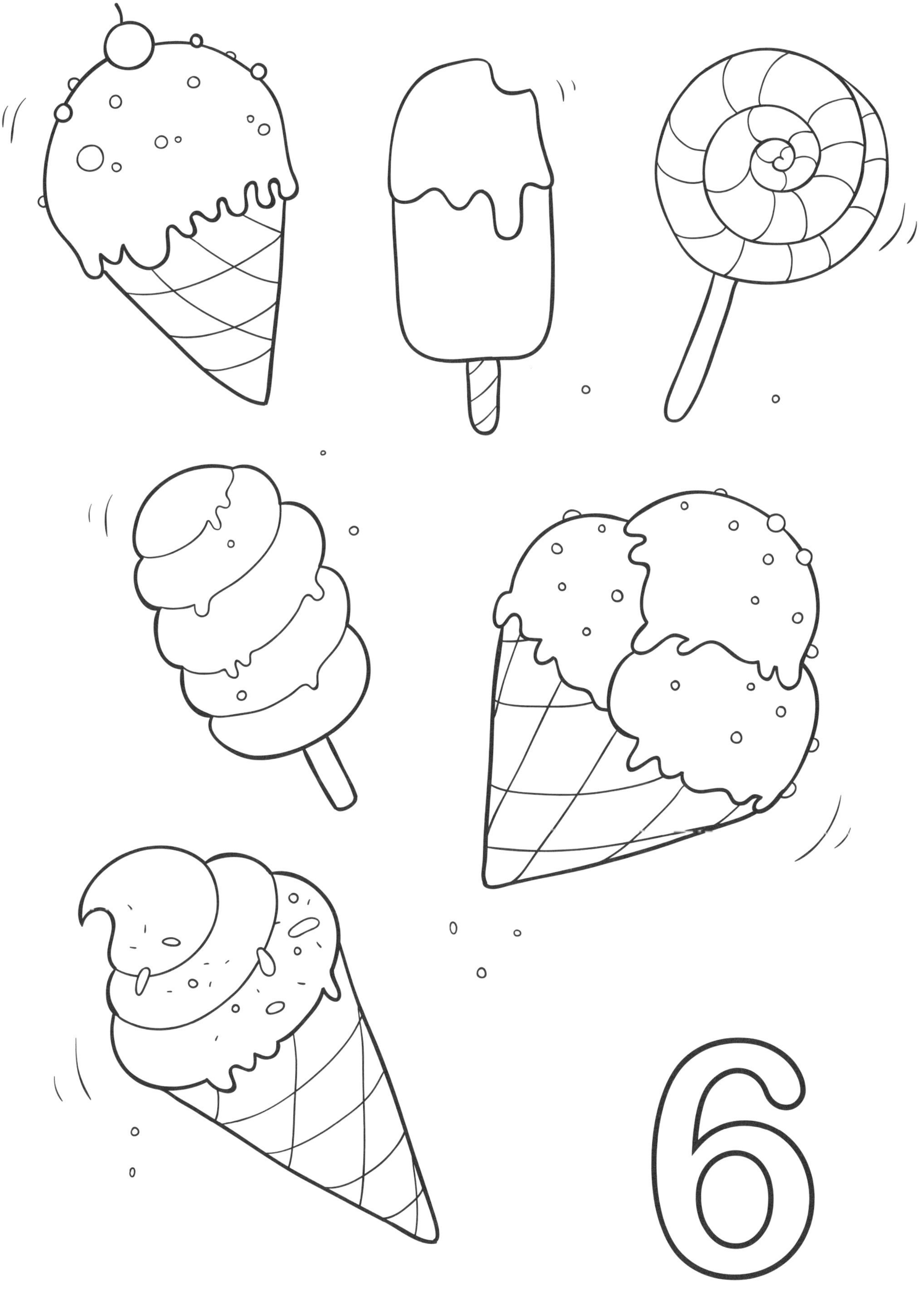
6

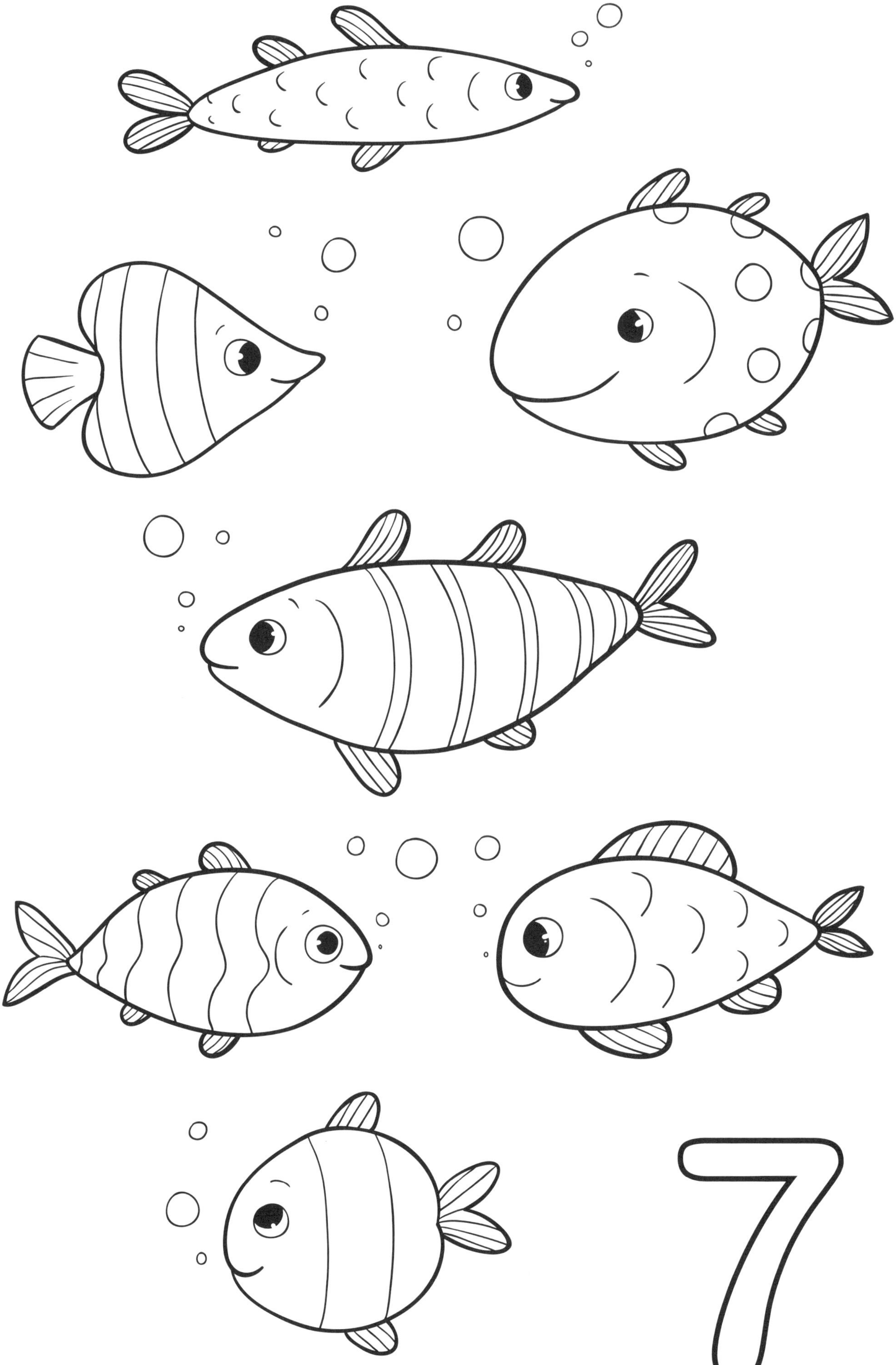
7

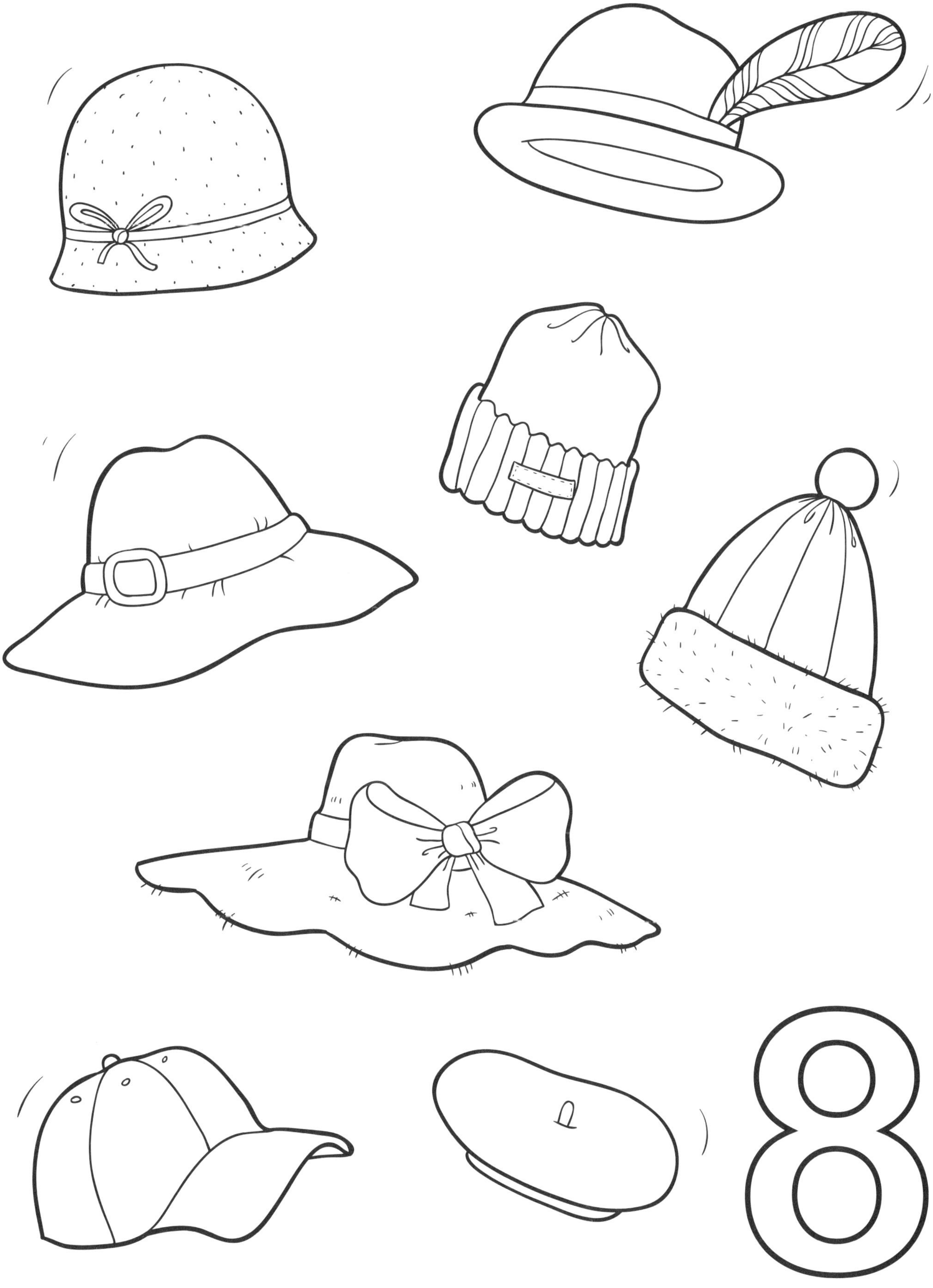
8

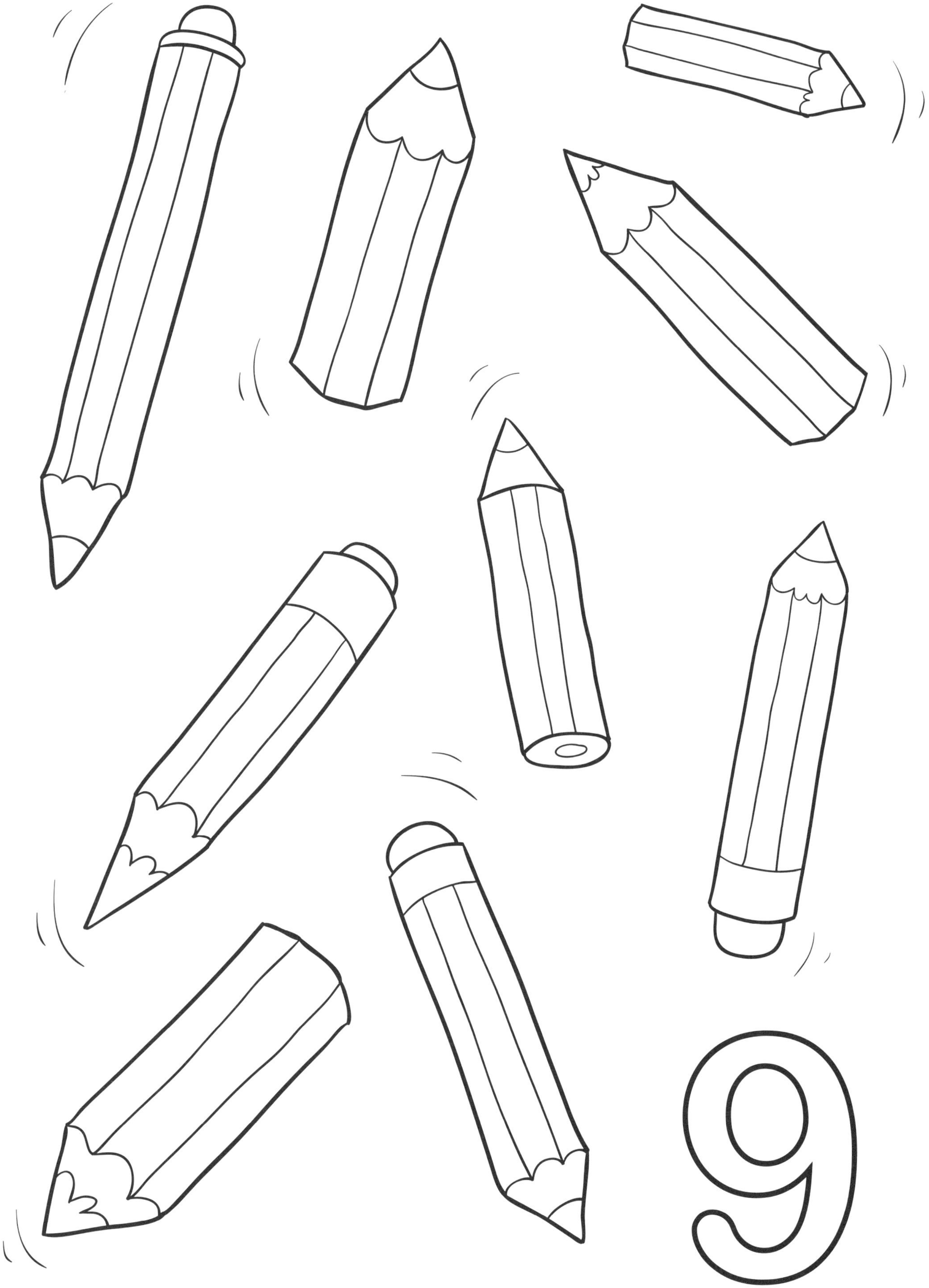

10

Numbers

0 1 2 3 4

5 6 7 8 9

10

Shapes

CIRCLE

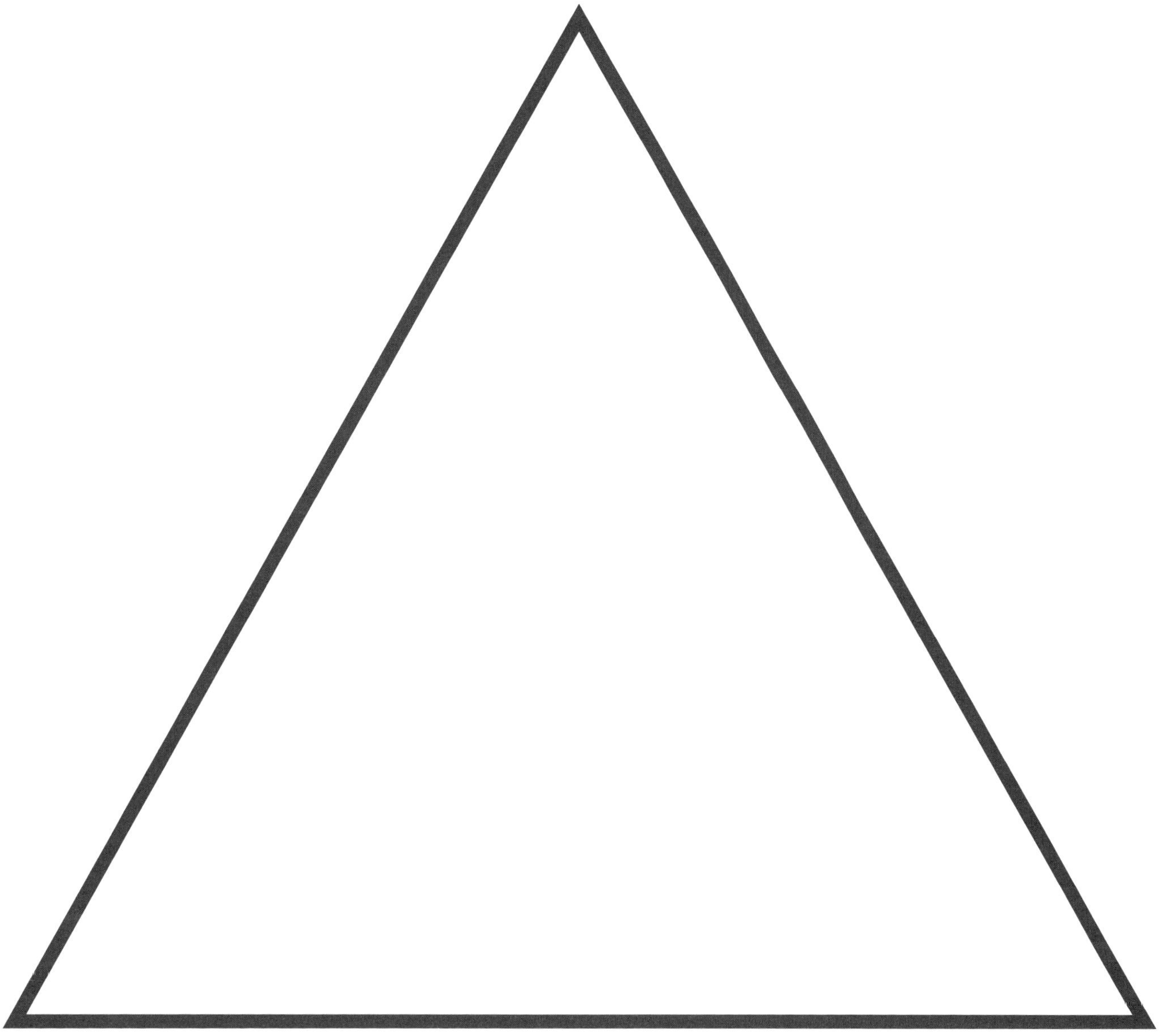

TRIANGLE

SQUARE

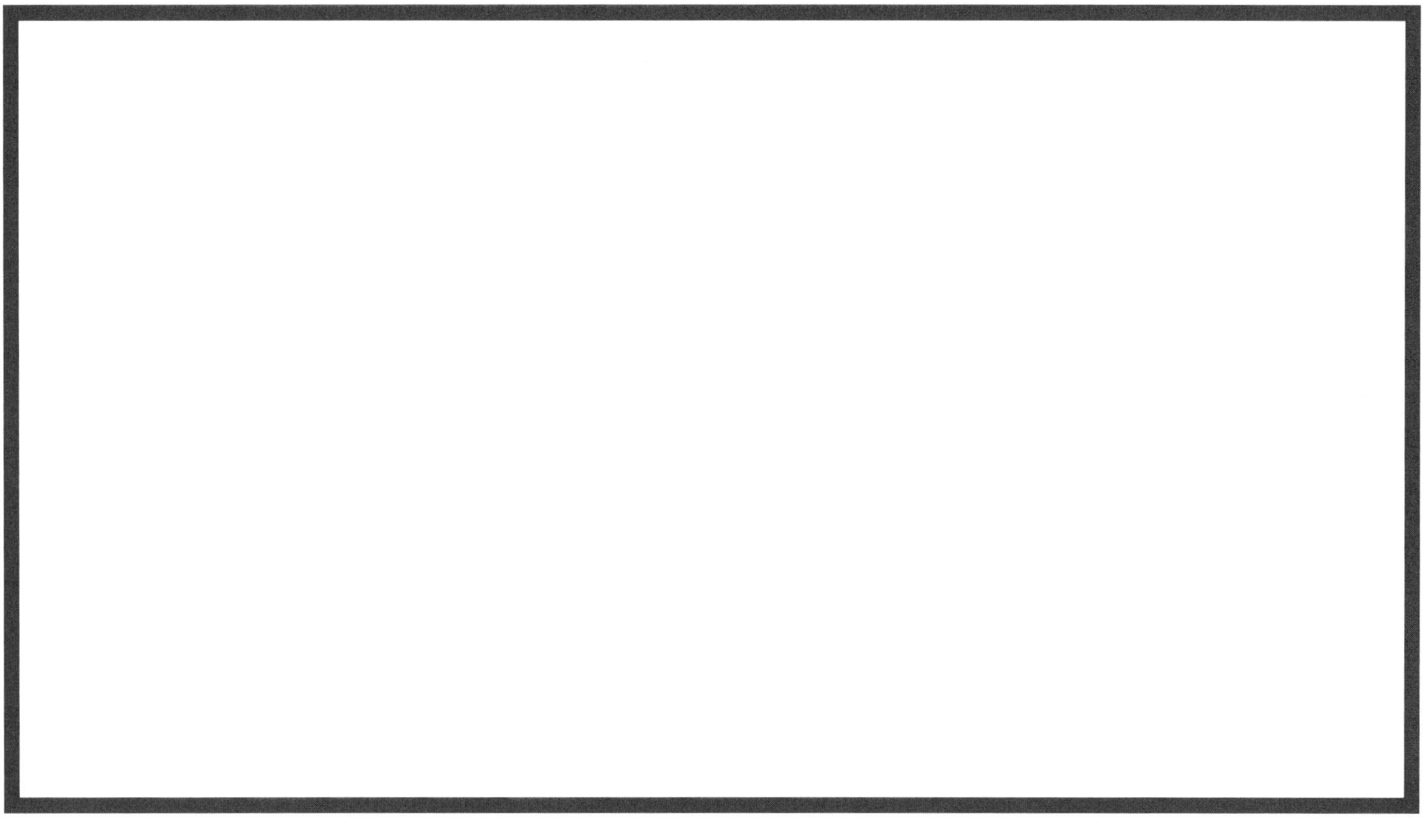

RECTANGLE

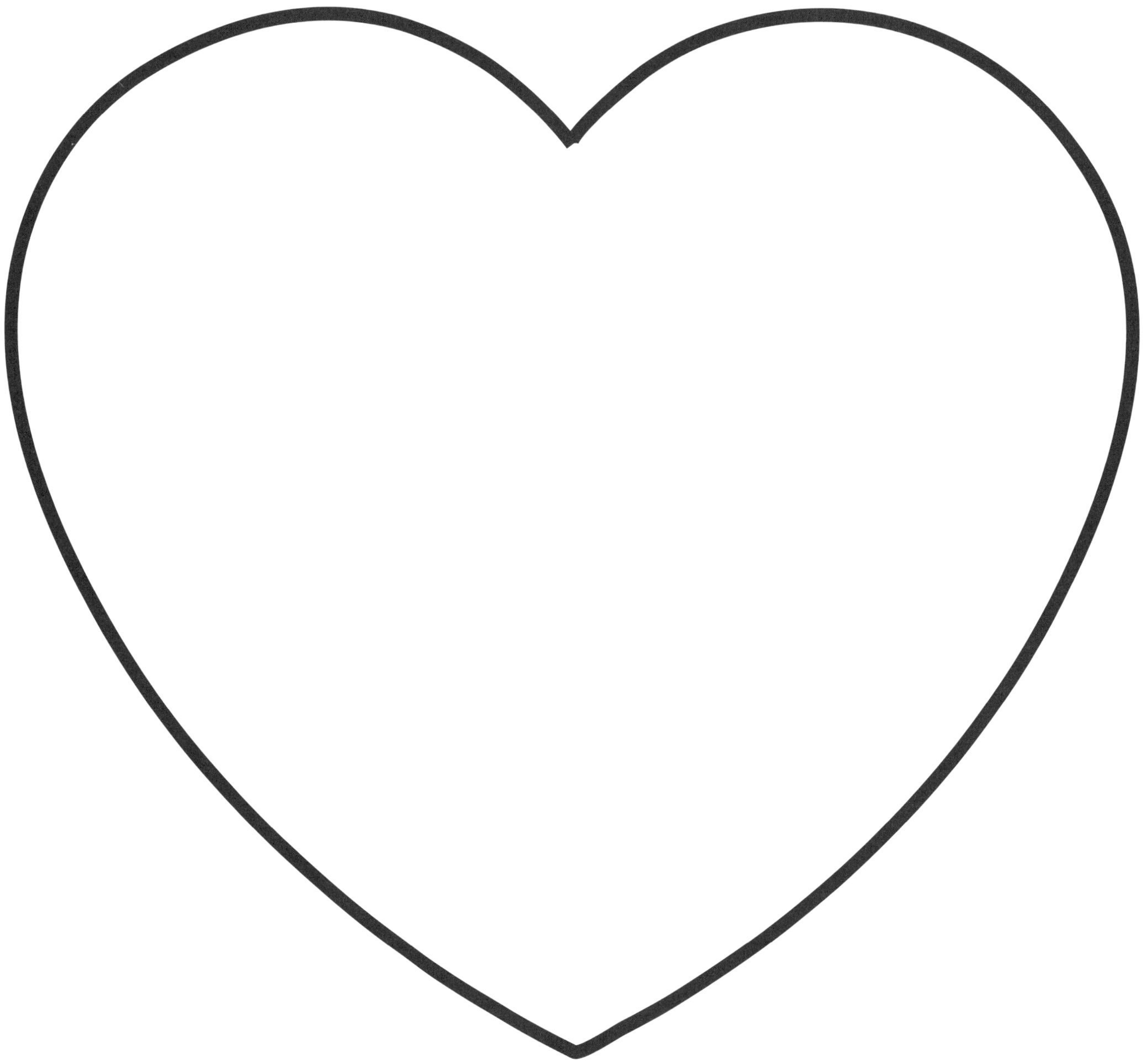

HEART

STAR

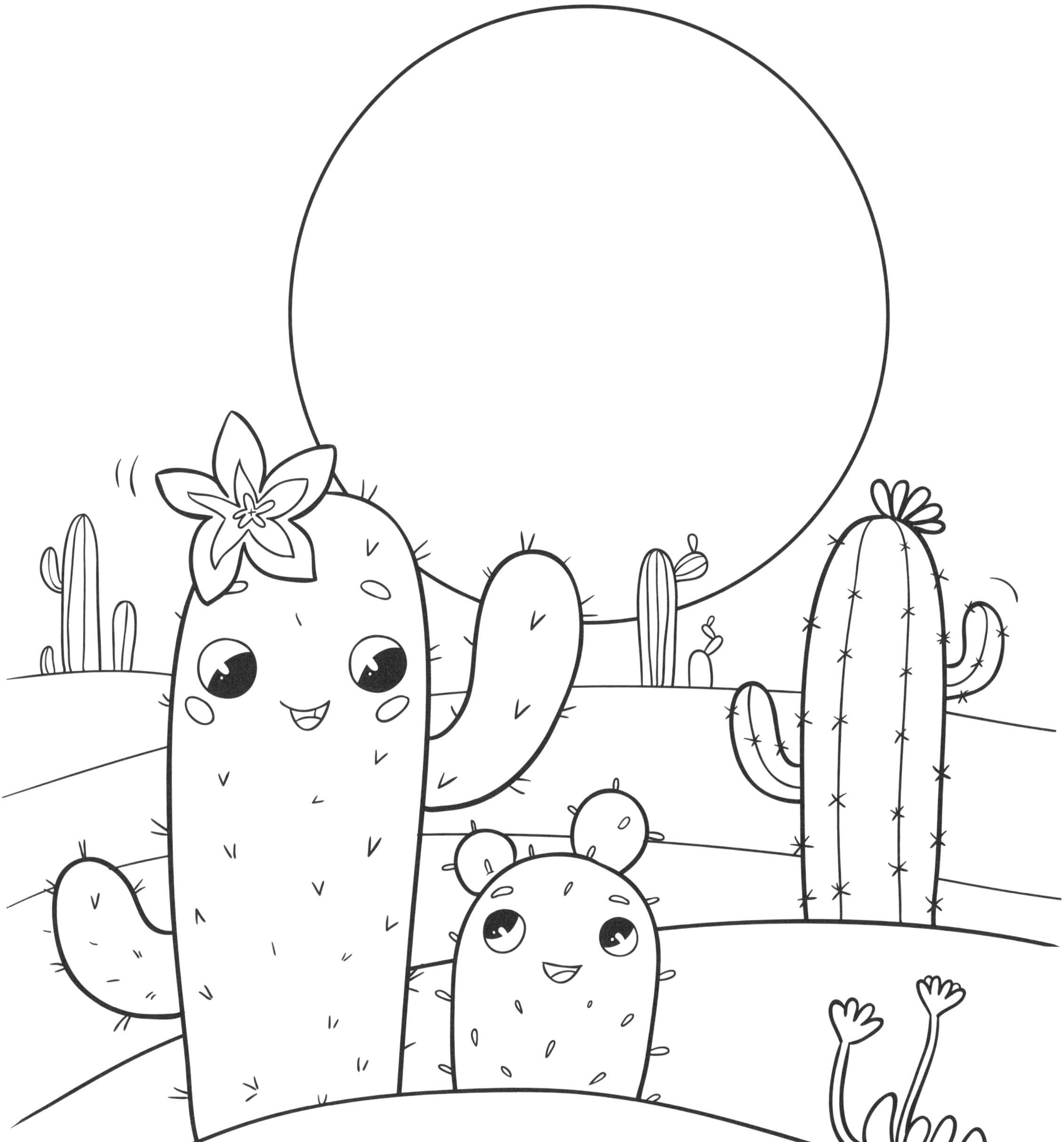

Circle

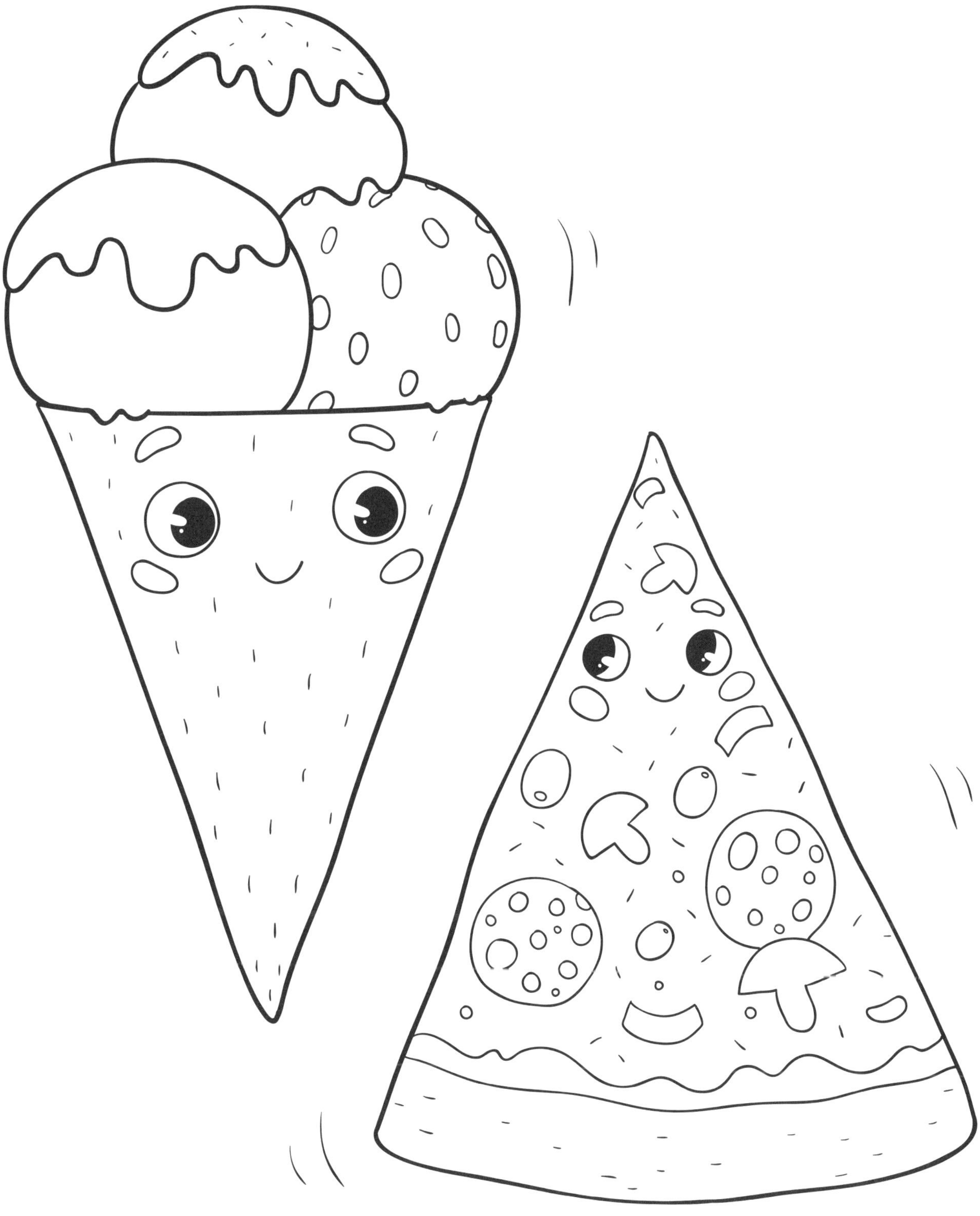

Triangle

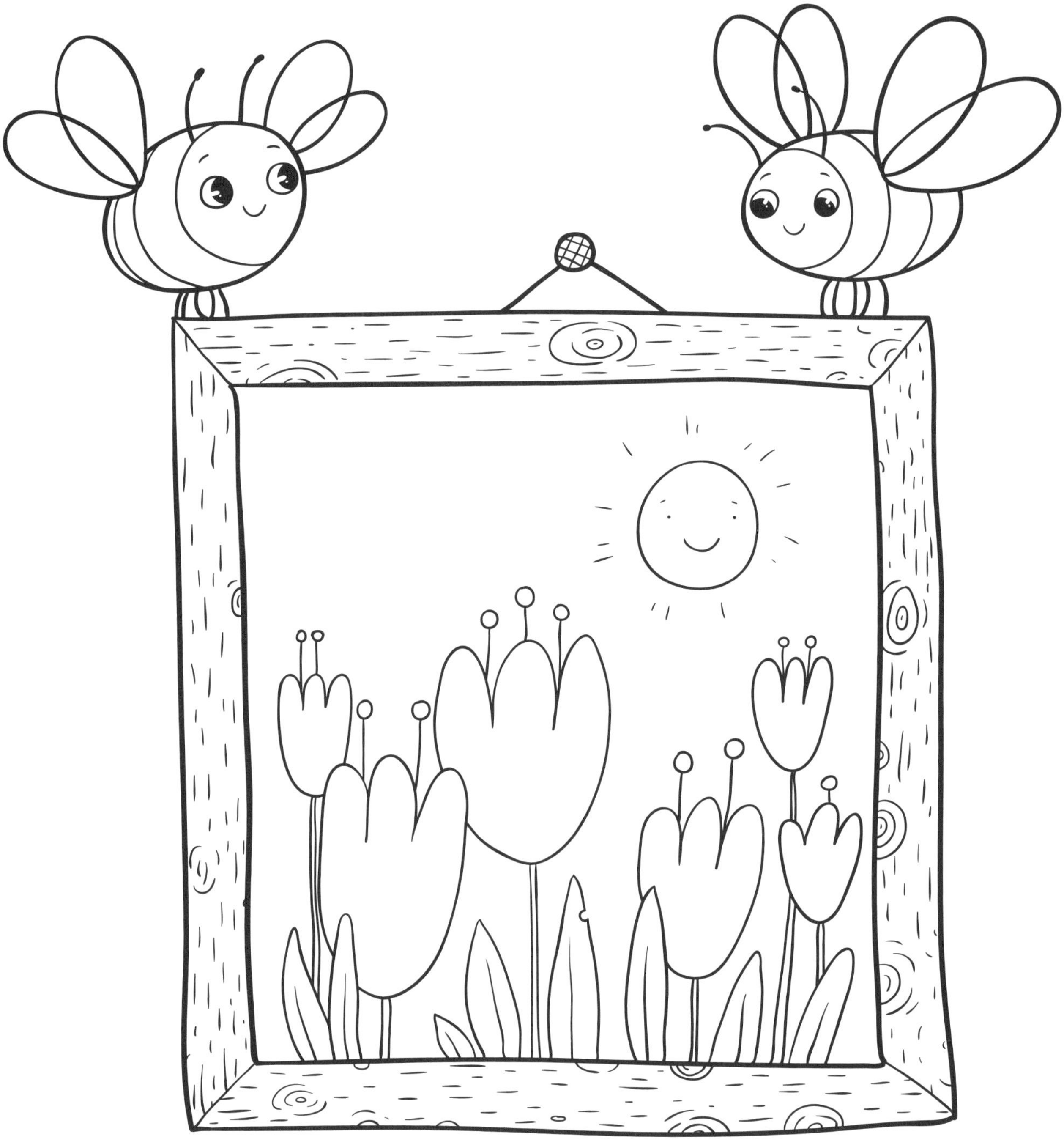

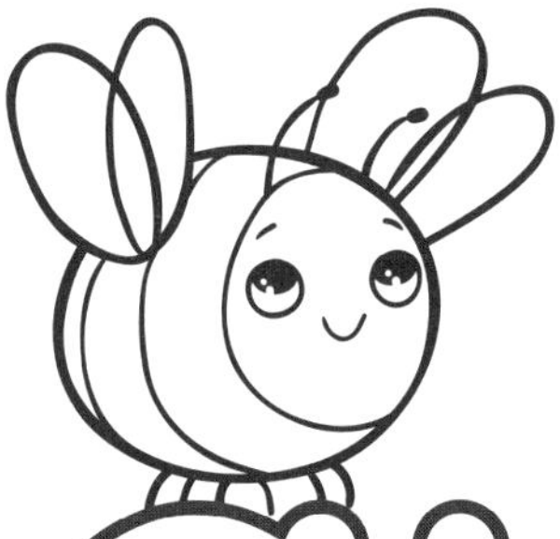

Square

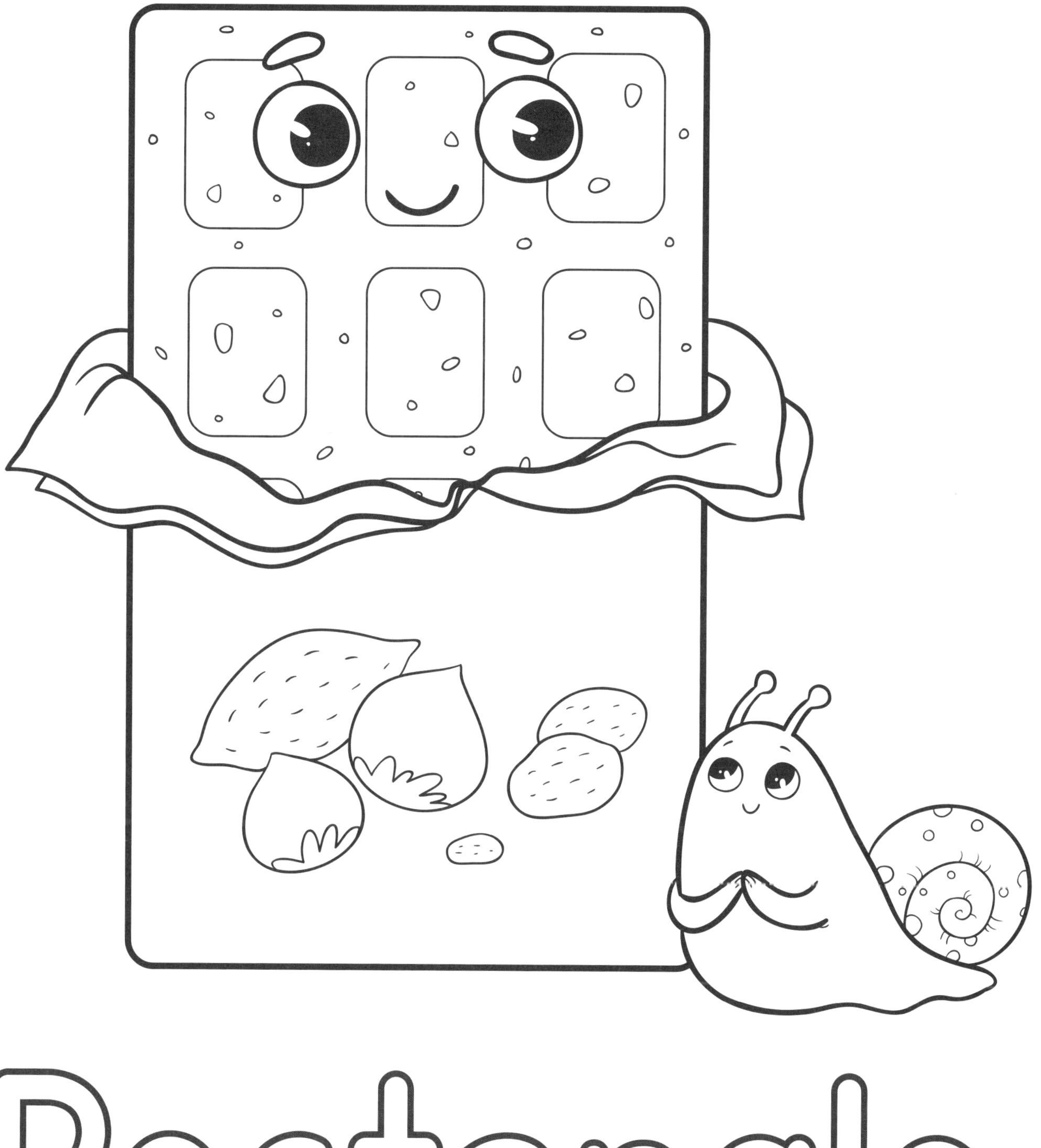

Rectangle

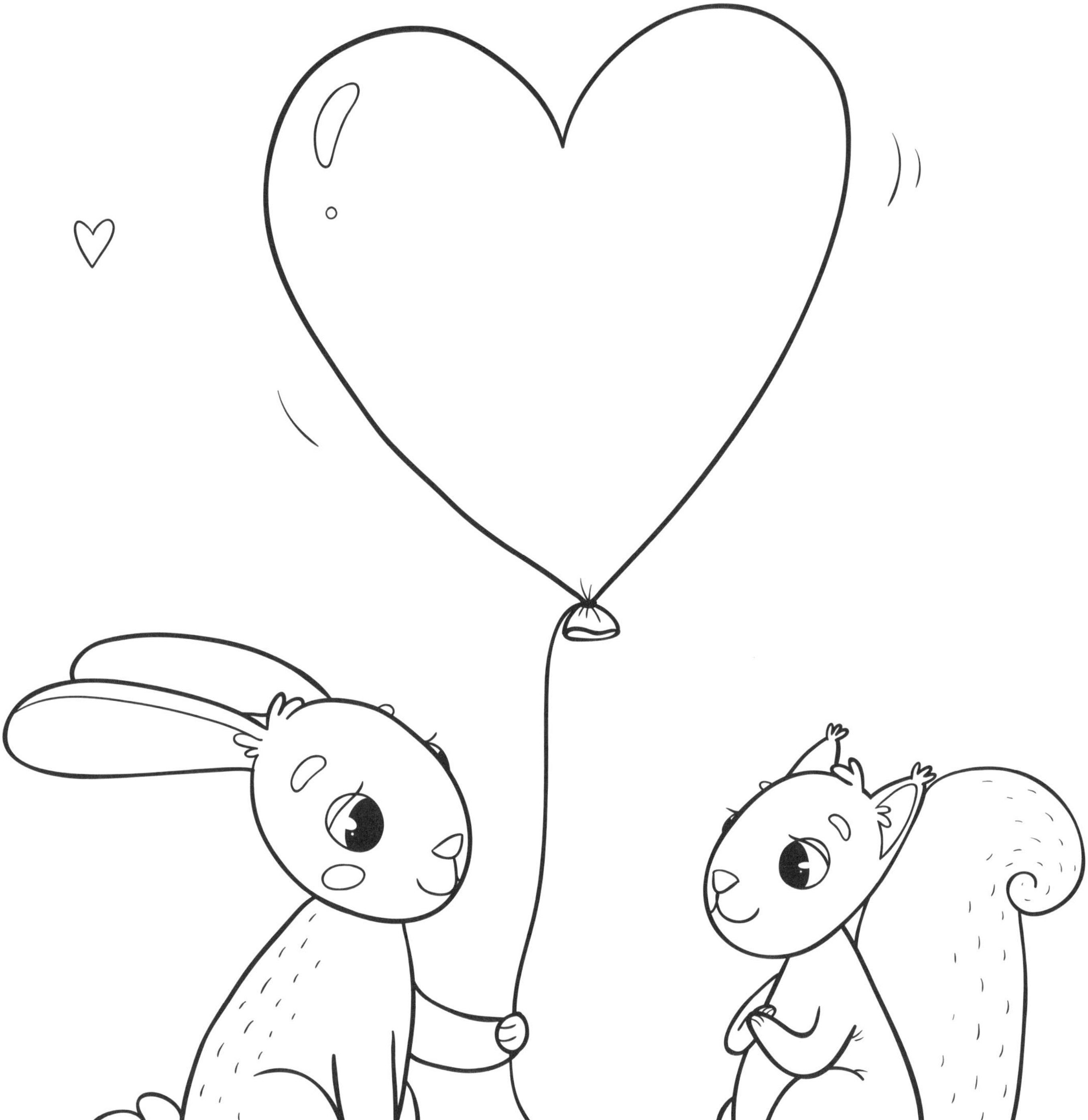

Heart

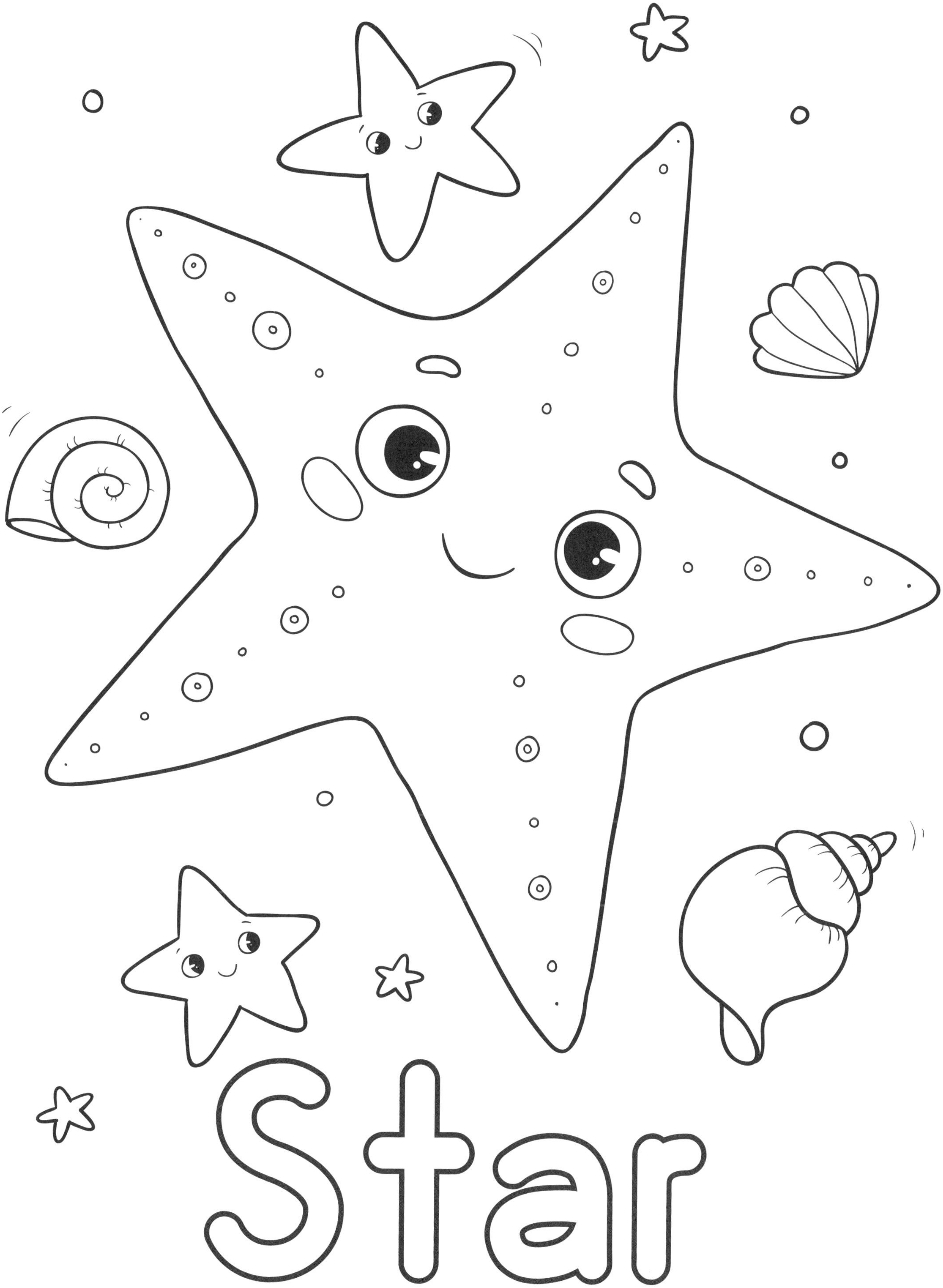
Star

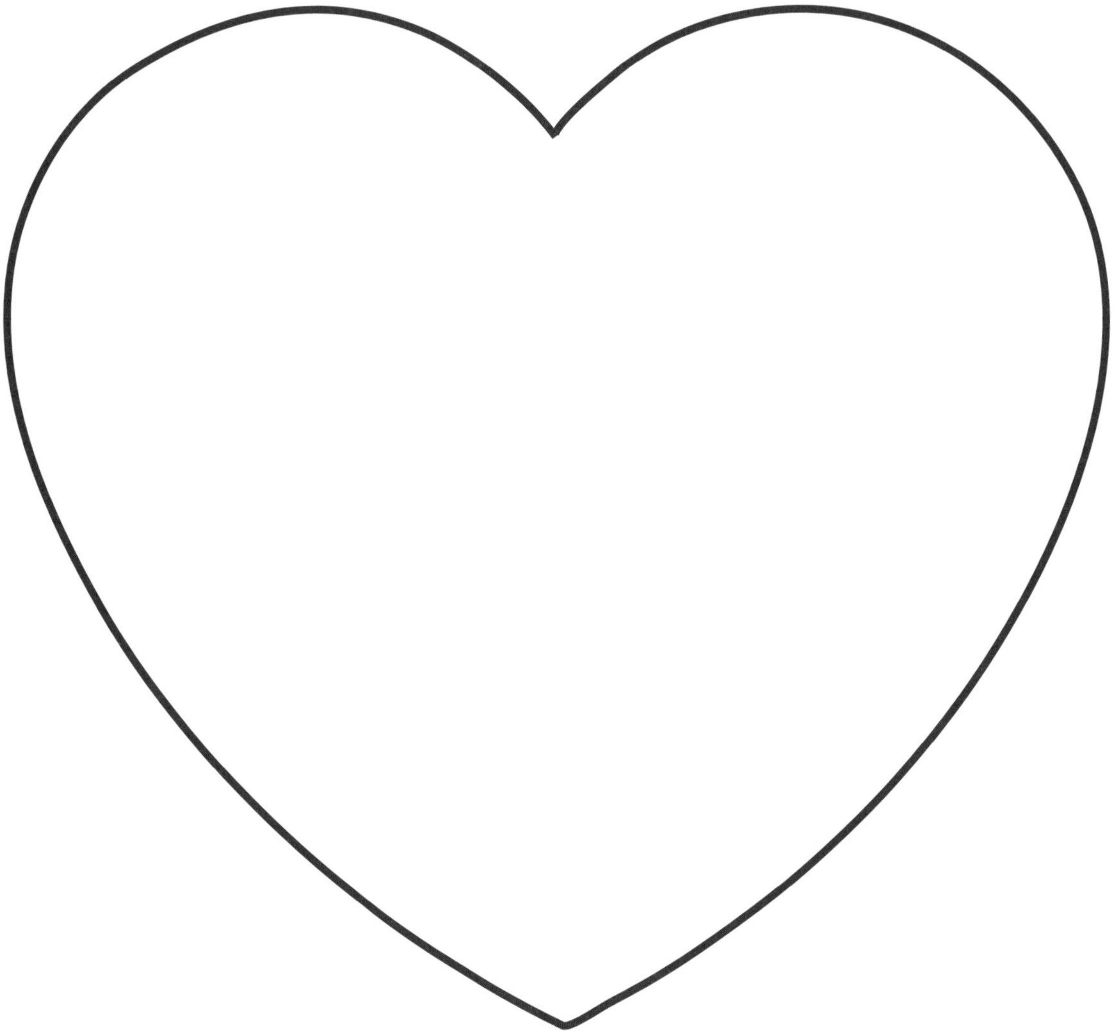

1 Heart

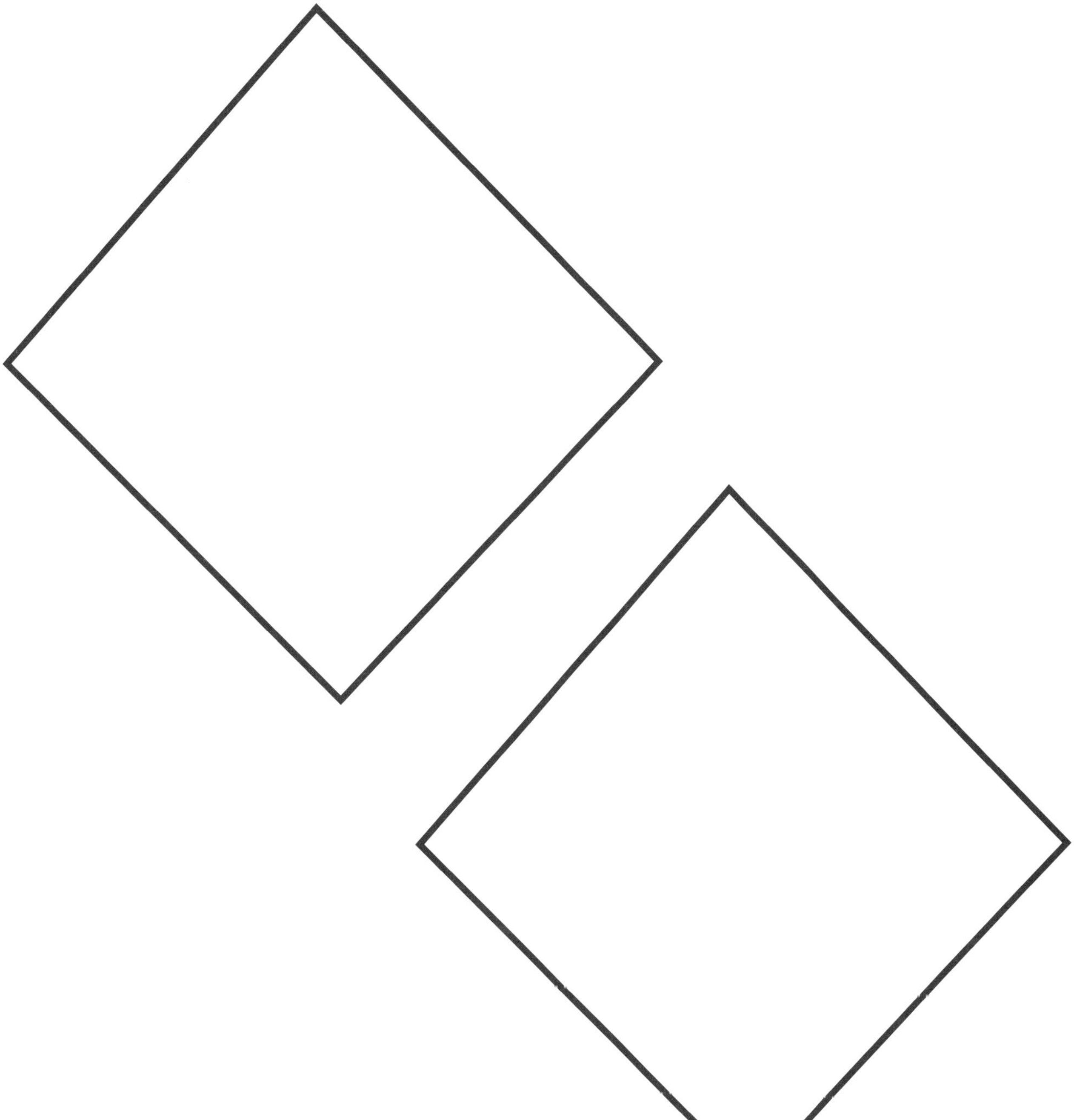

2 Diamonds

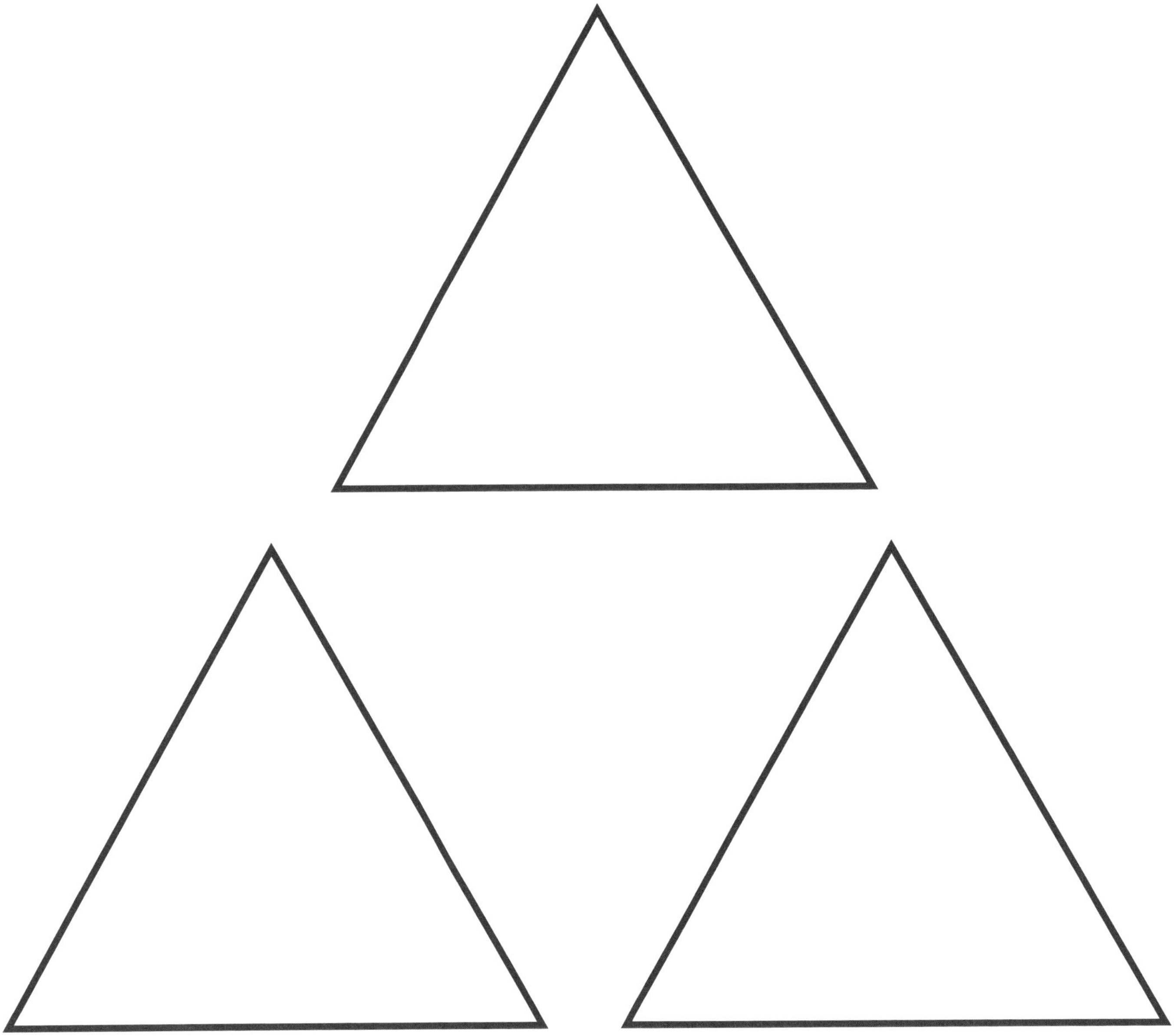

3 Triangles

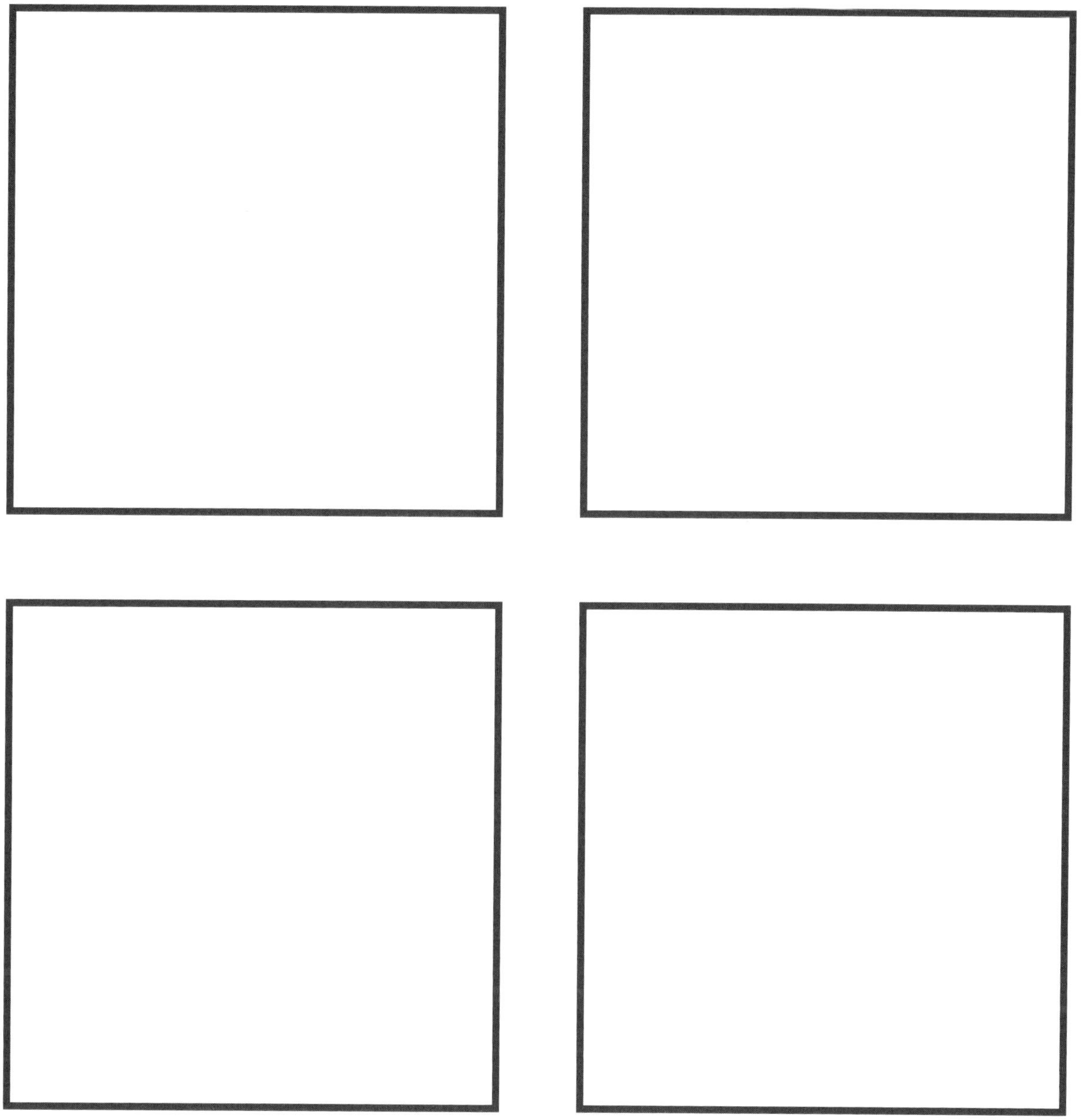

4 Squares

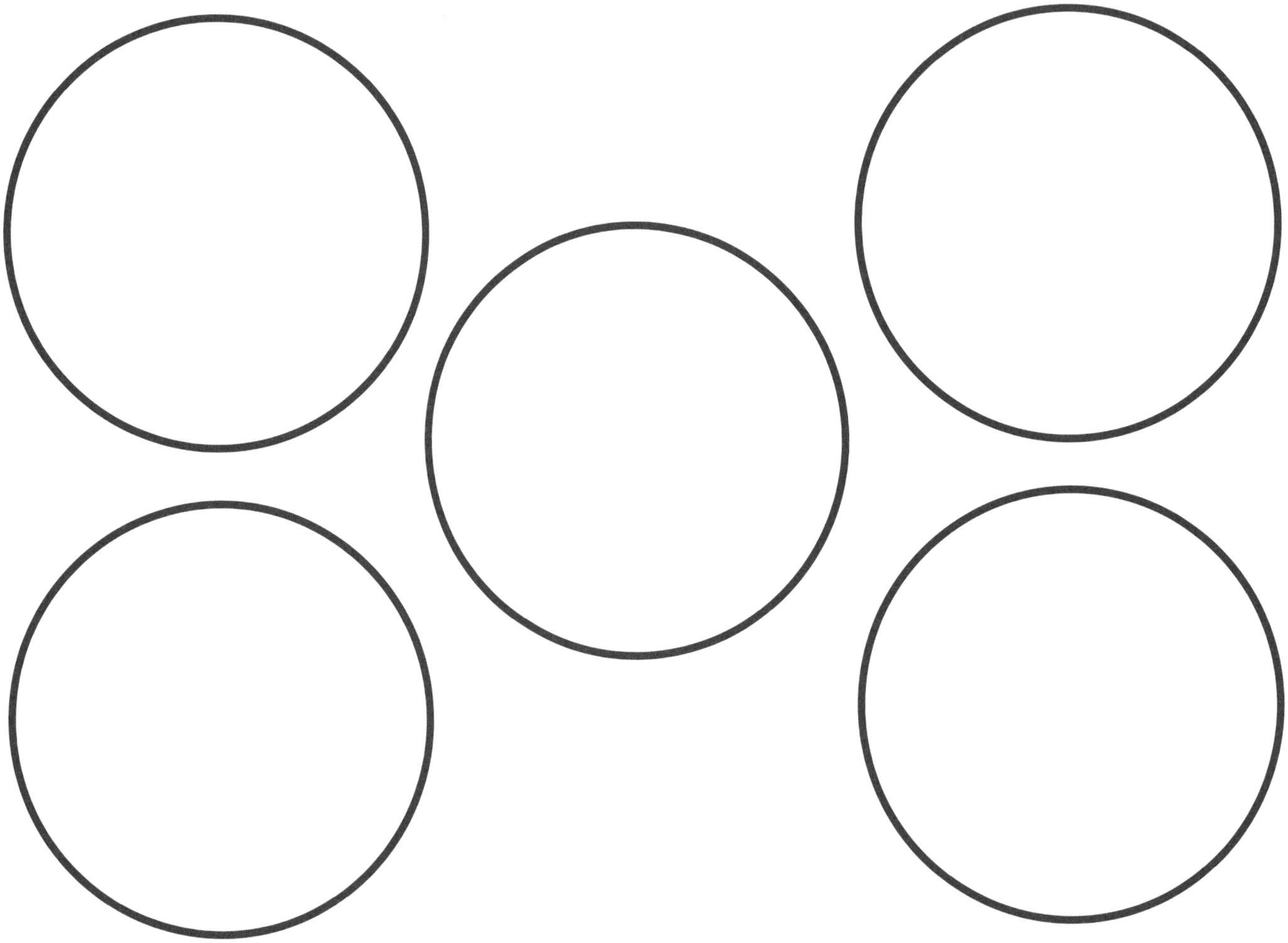

5 Circles

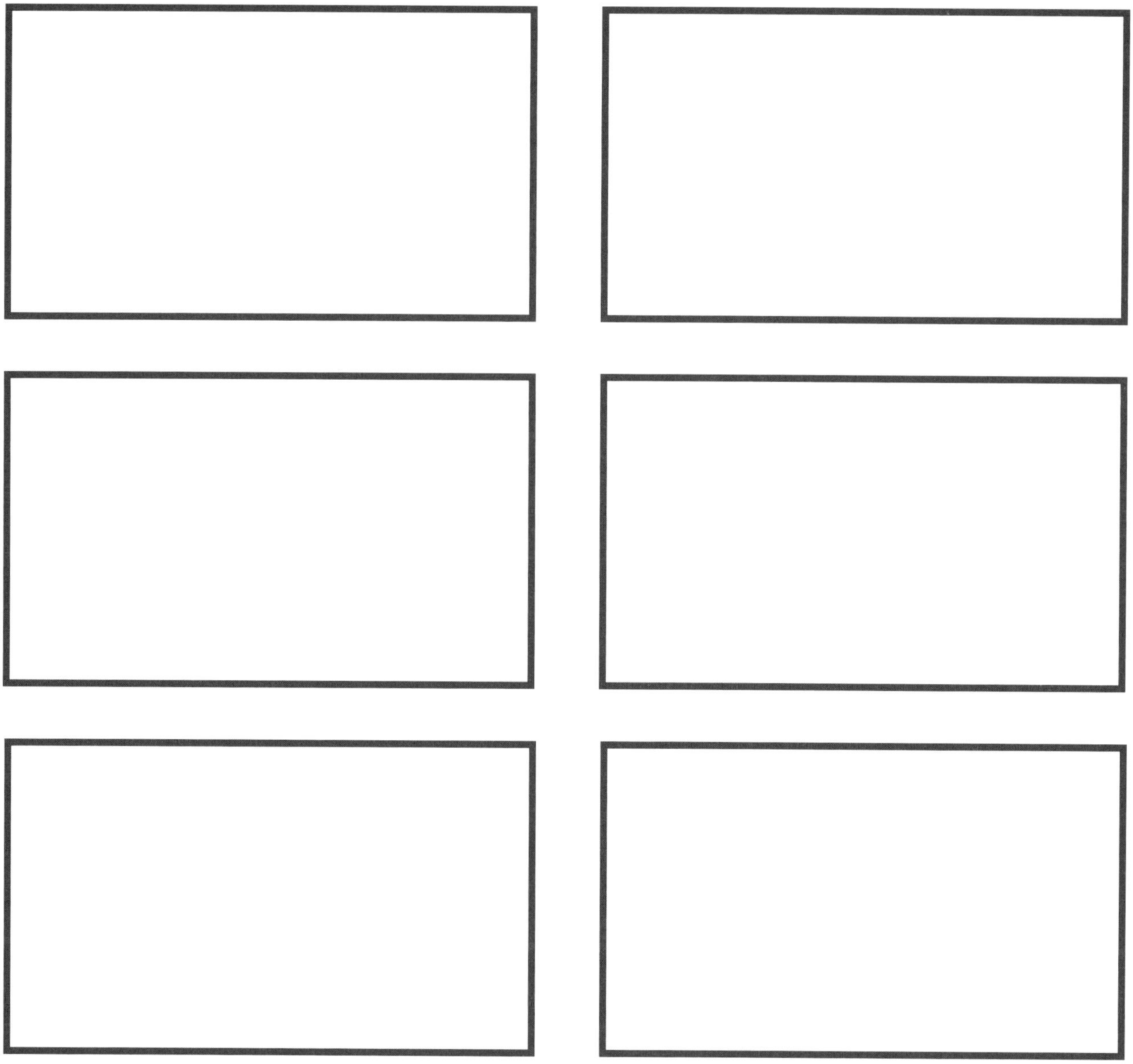

6 Rectangles

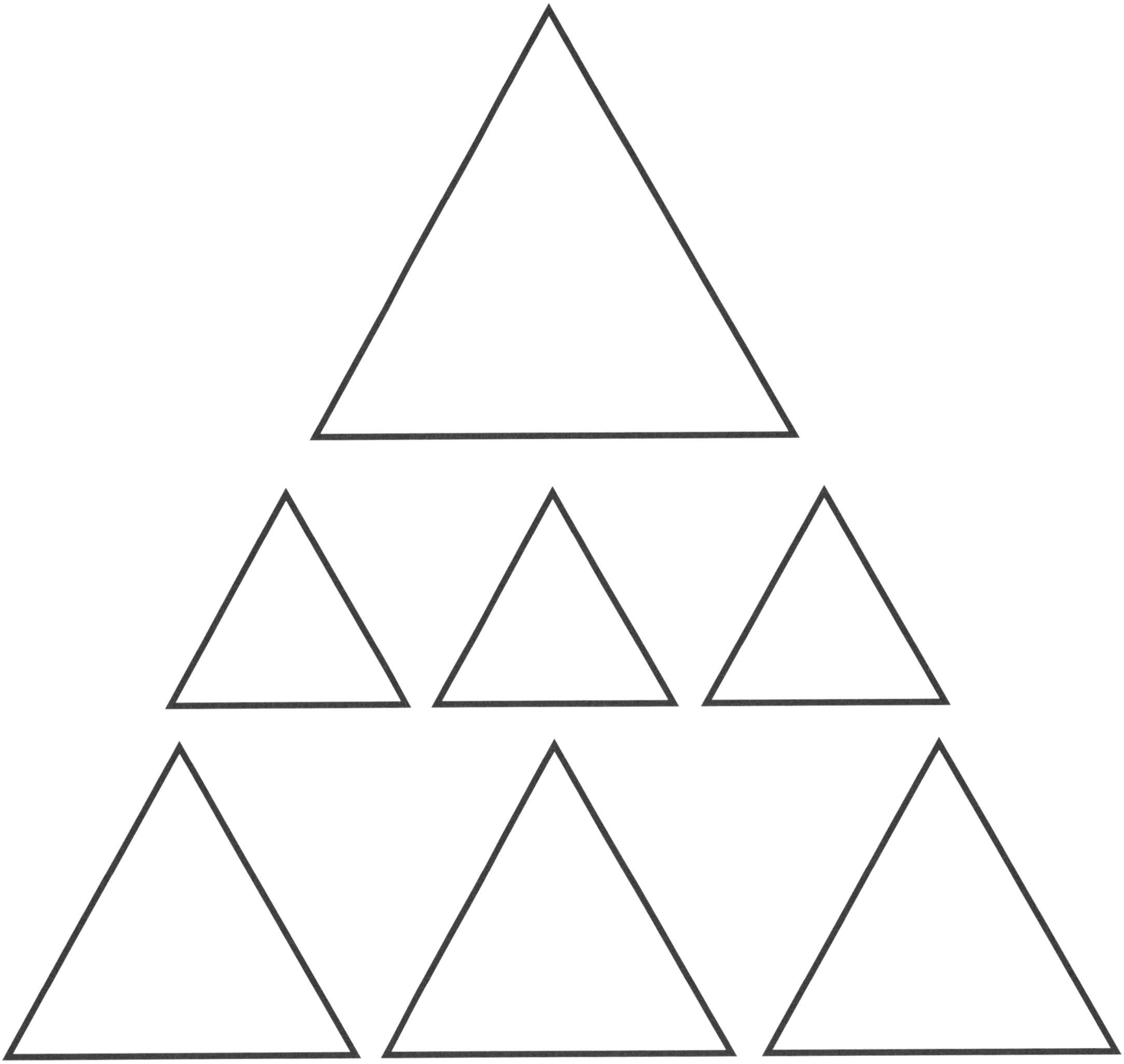

7 Triangles

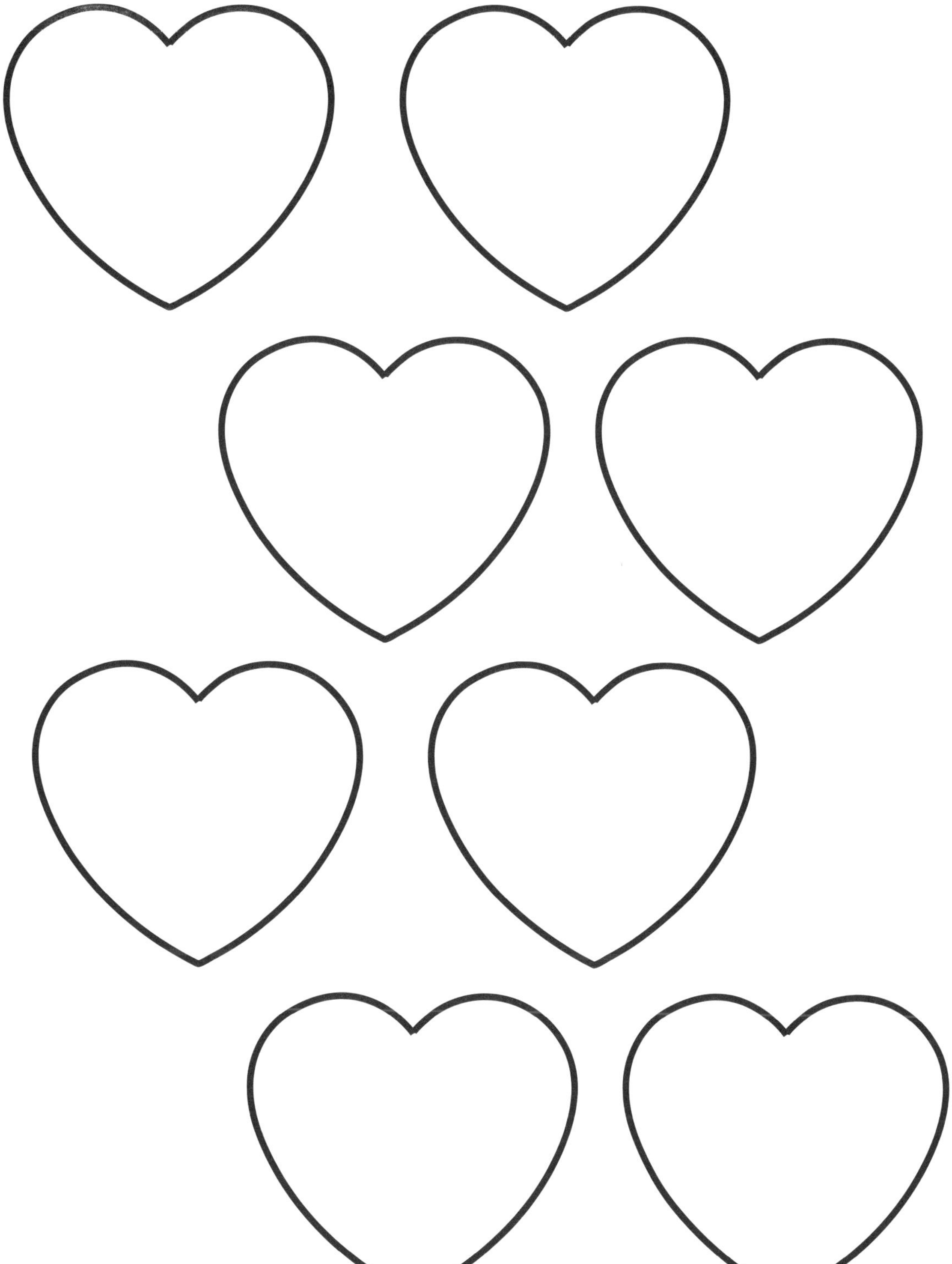

8 Hearts

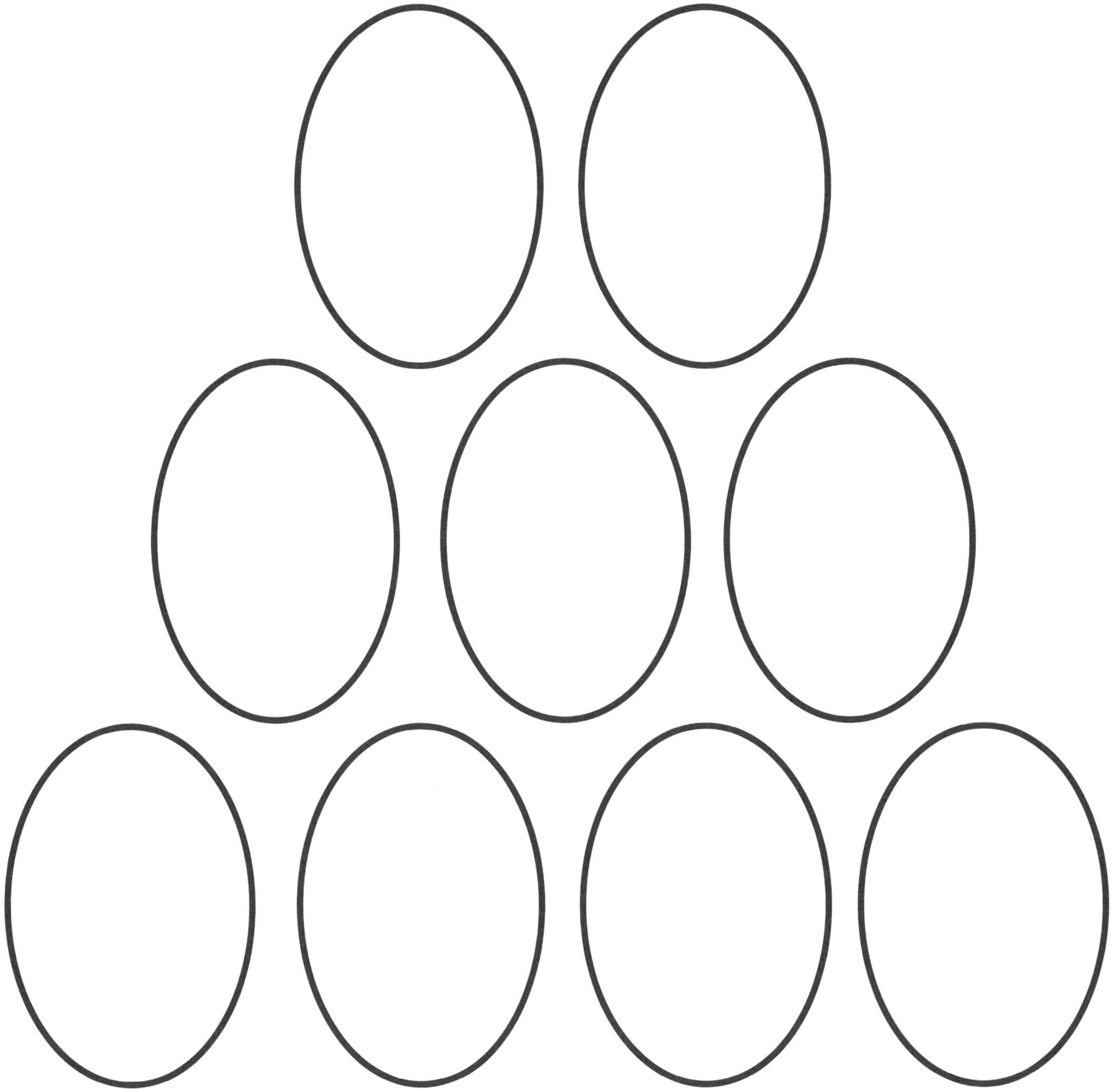

9 Ovals

10 Stars

Shapes

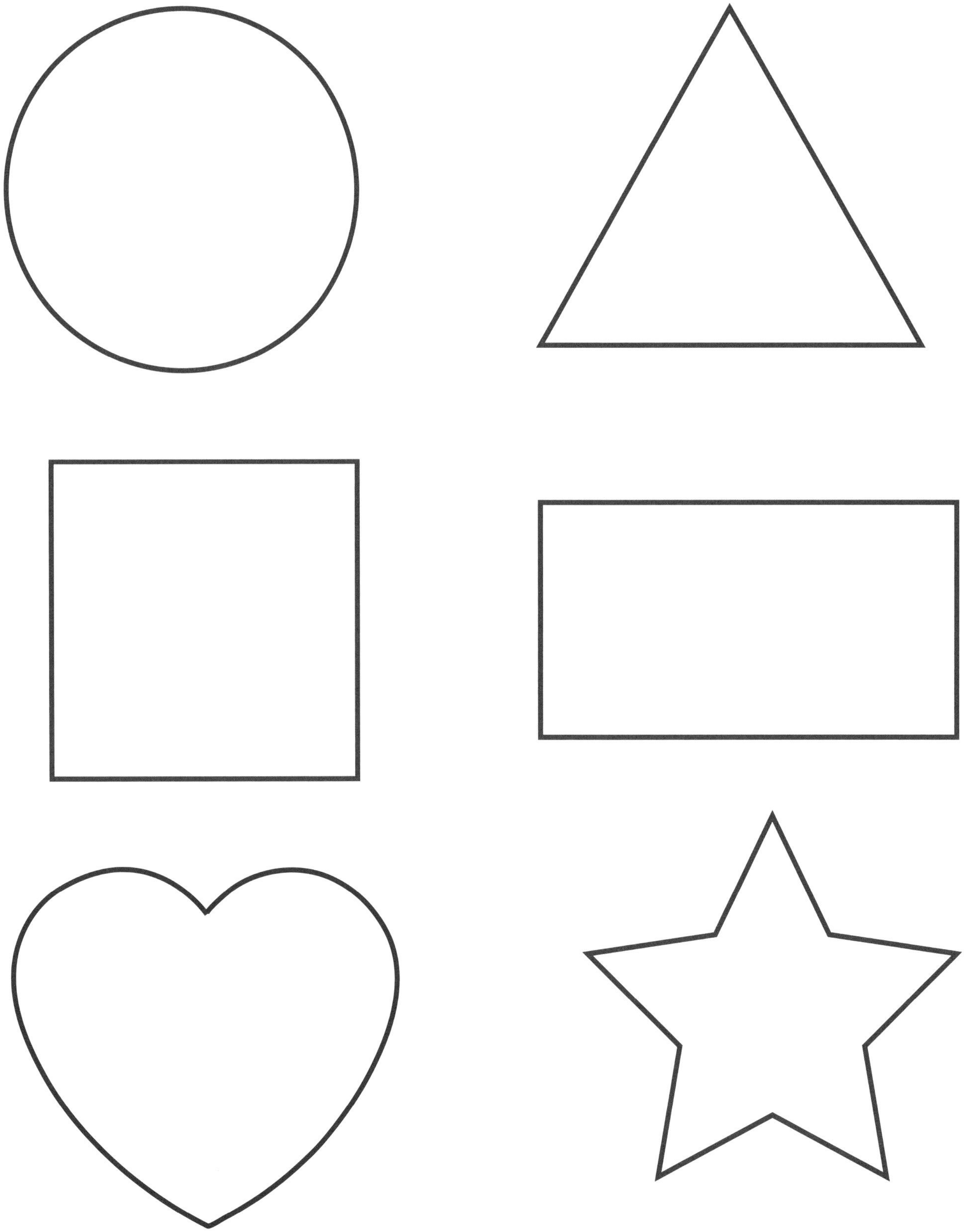

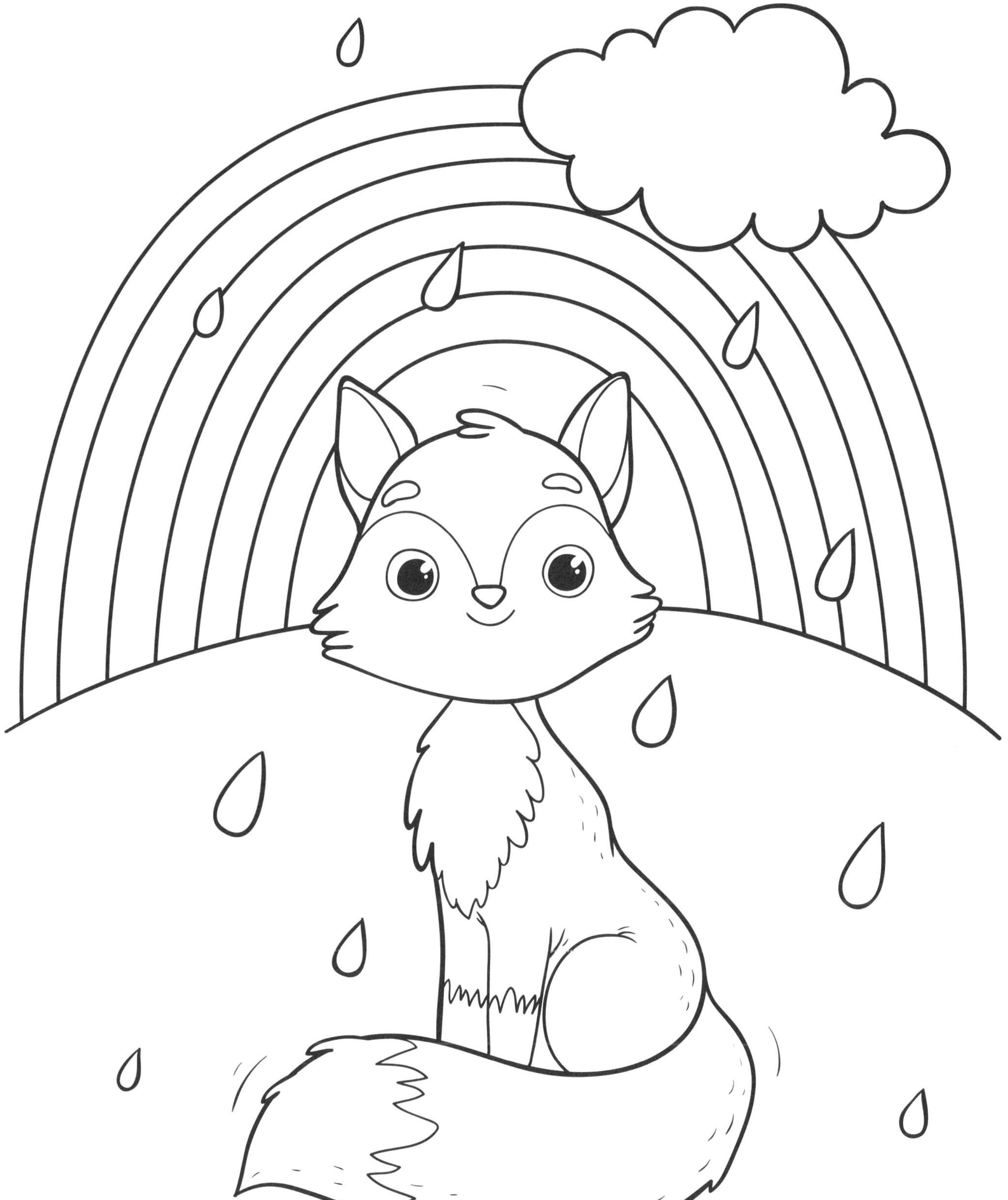

Colors

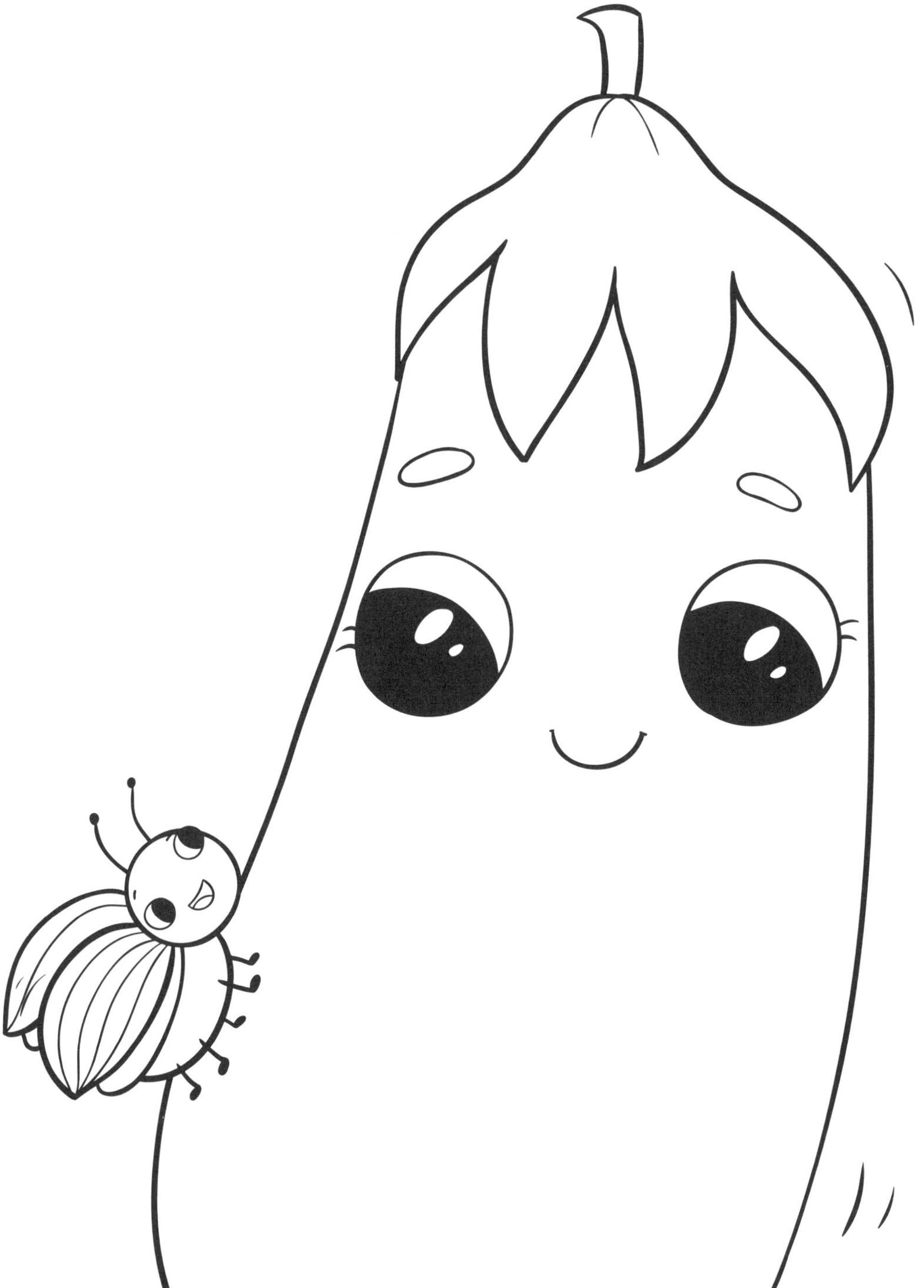

Violet

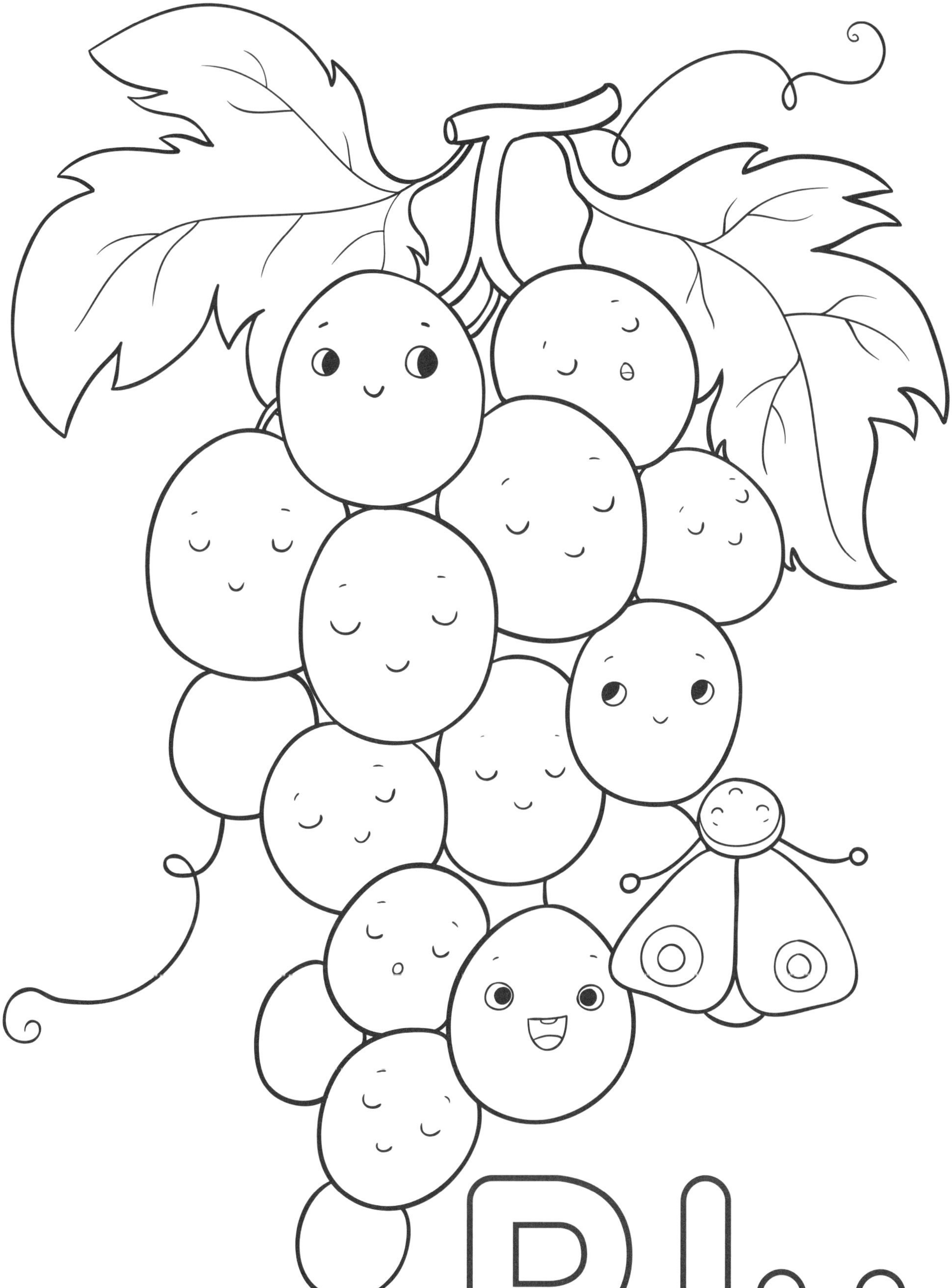

Blue

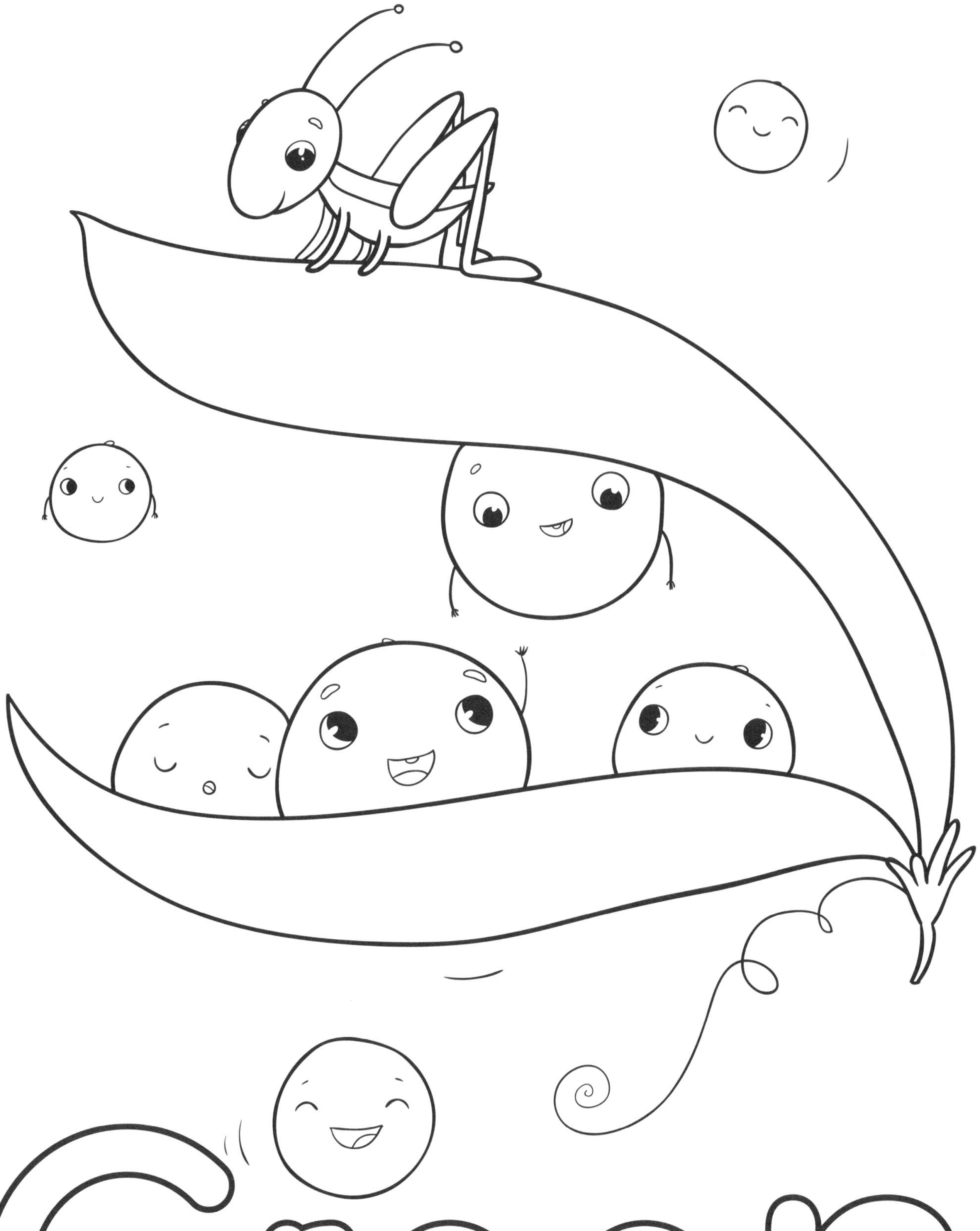

Green

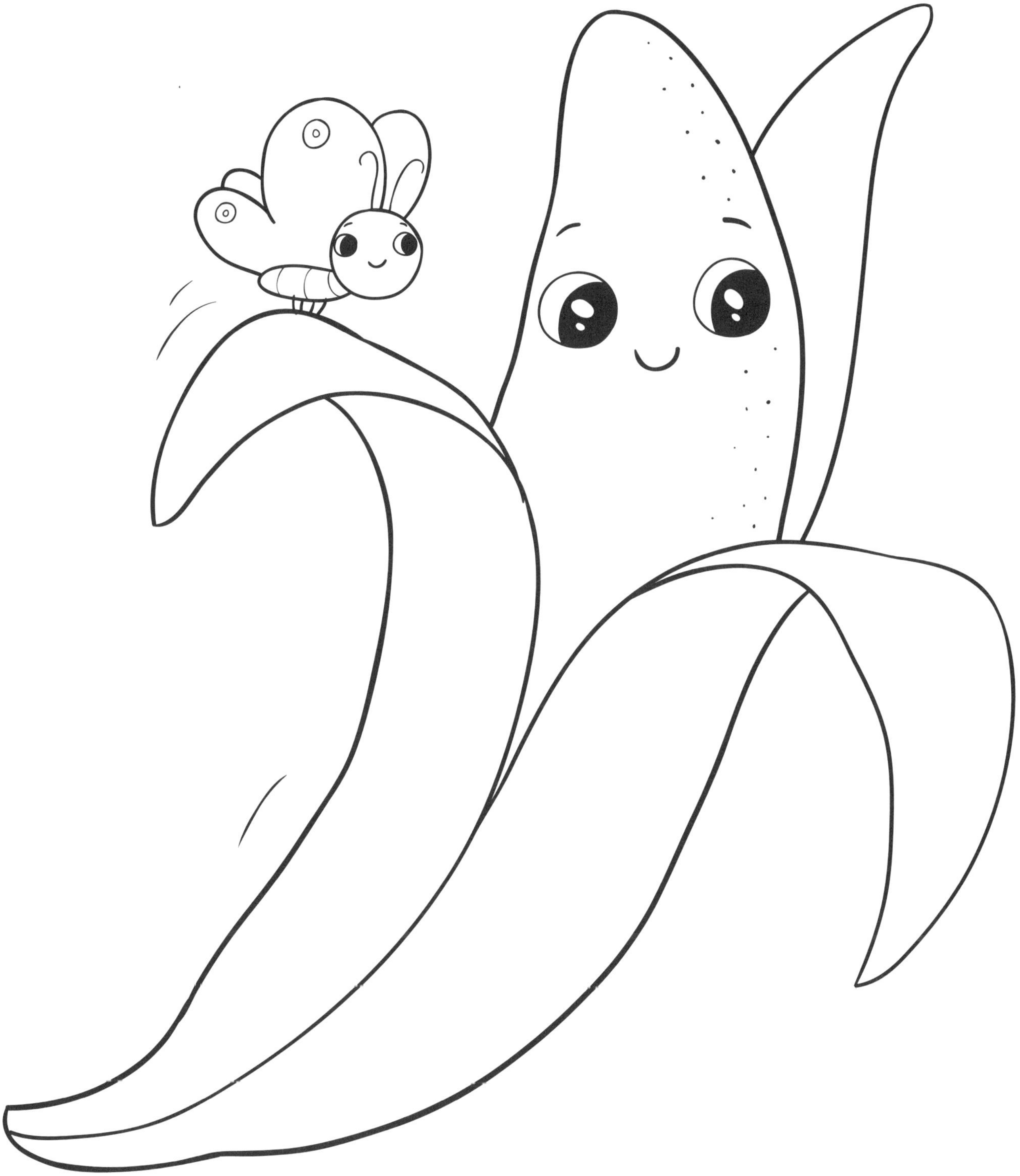

Yellow

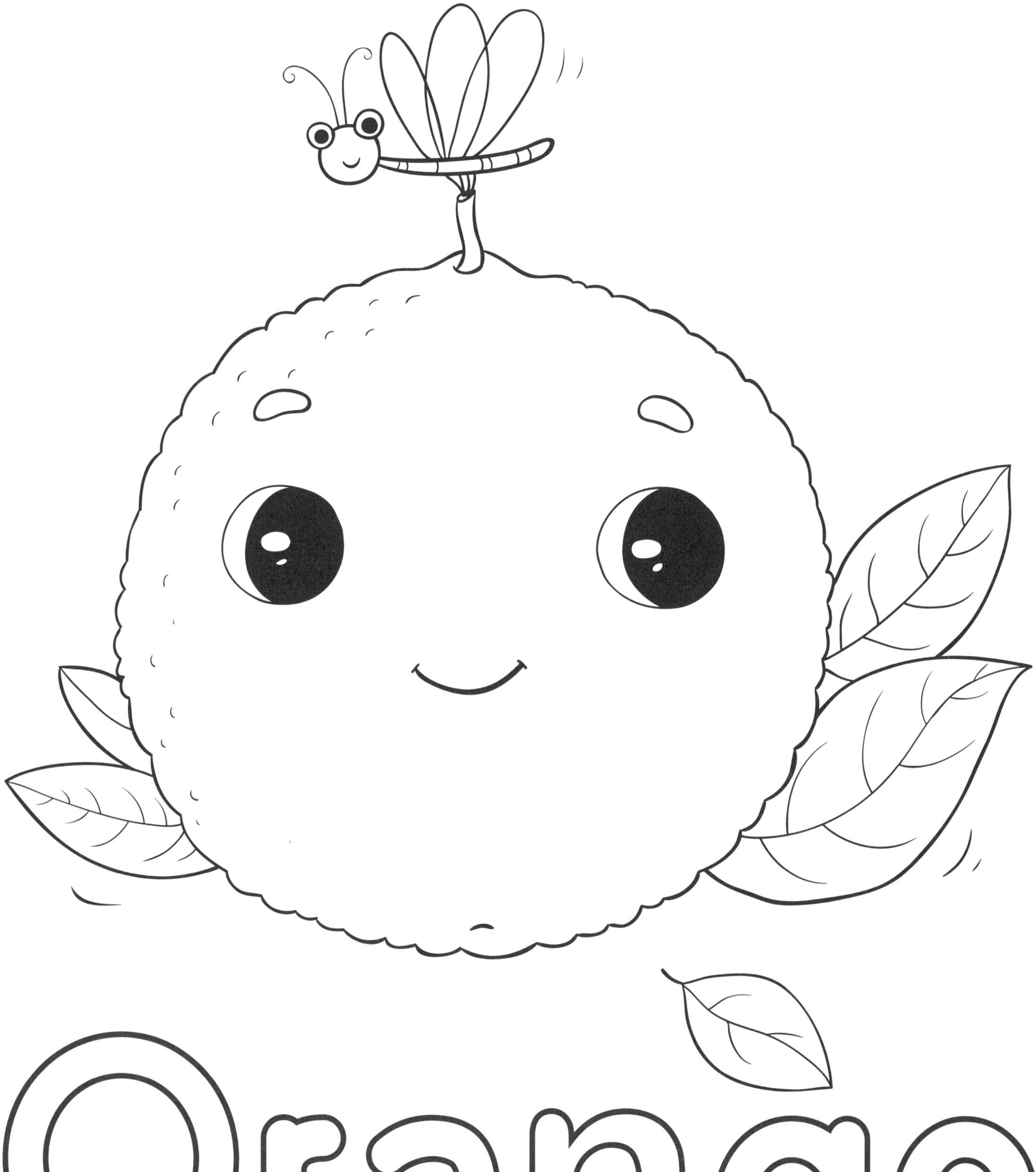

Orange

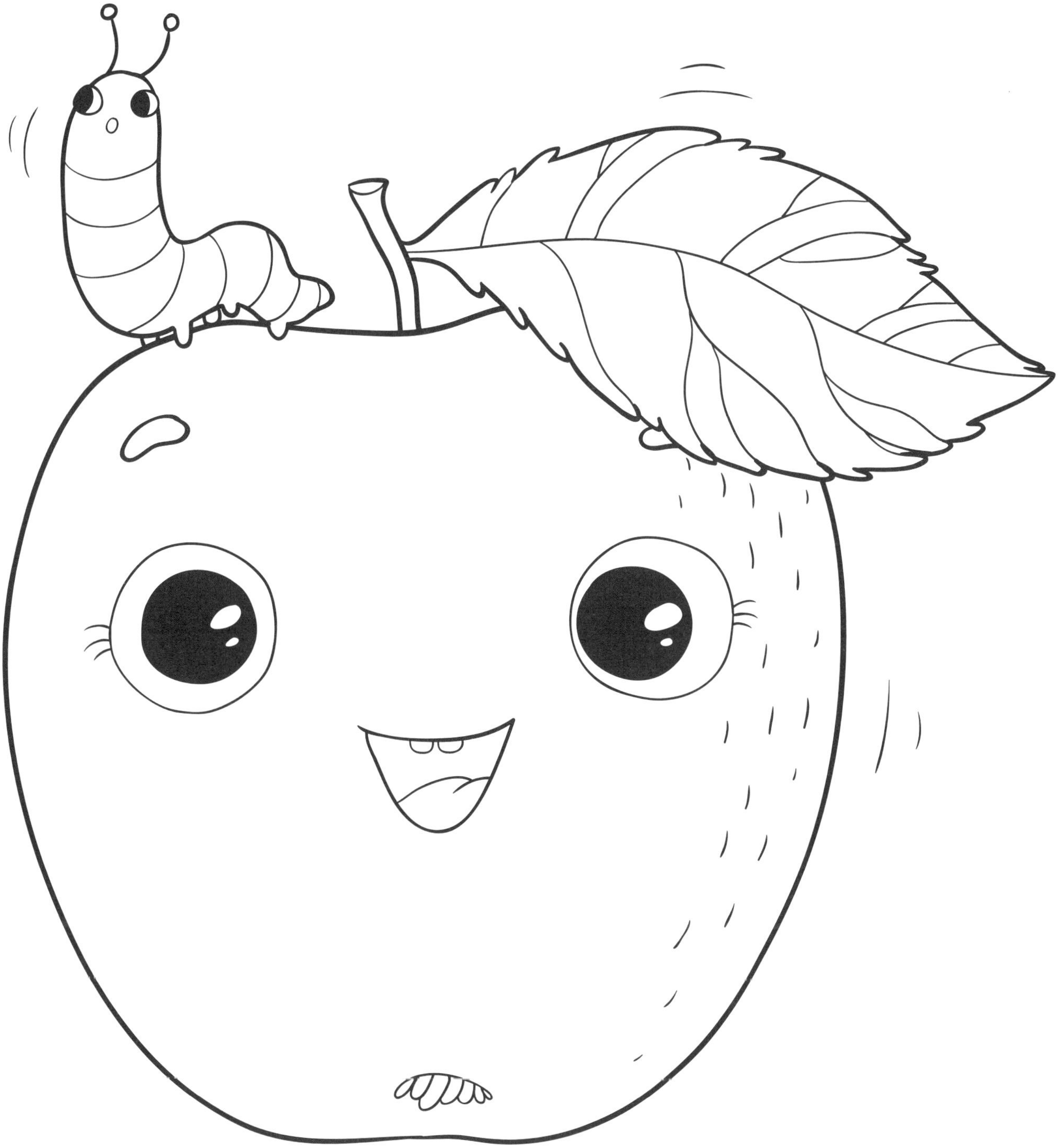

Red

Colors

Violet

Blue

Green

Yellow

Orange

Red

Thank You so Much

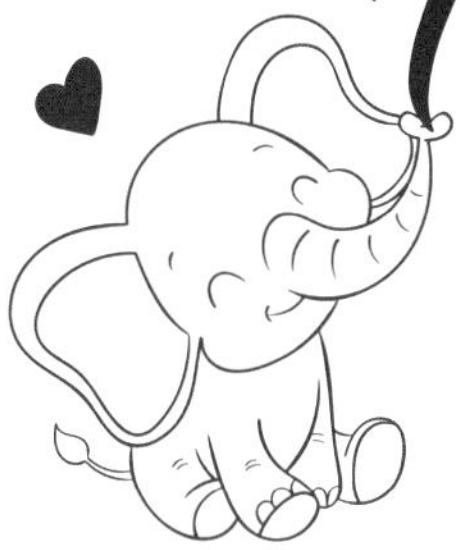

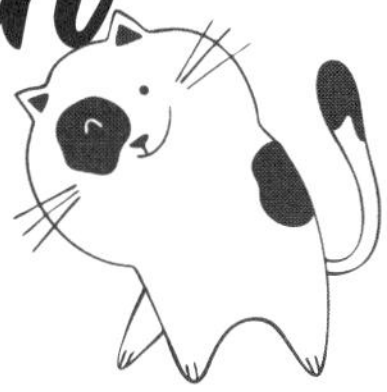

There are a lot of choices out there but you chose us when you bought this book. This means the world to us. We wish to express our gratitude for your purchase.

If you or your family enjoyed using this book, we request that you please visit your order history on Amazon and leave us a review with your honest opinion. It will only take a few minutes, but all feedback is valued and appreciated.

As a small token of thanks for buying our book, we have added two additional doodle pages with positive affirmation quotes to help reinforce positive thinking in your children while they color. Please enjoy

We hope to be the brand you first think of the next time you look for the best creative activity book for your kids.

Thank you for your support. You're the best!

If you liked the book, please refer it to your friends and family.

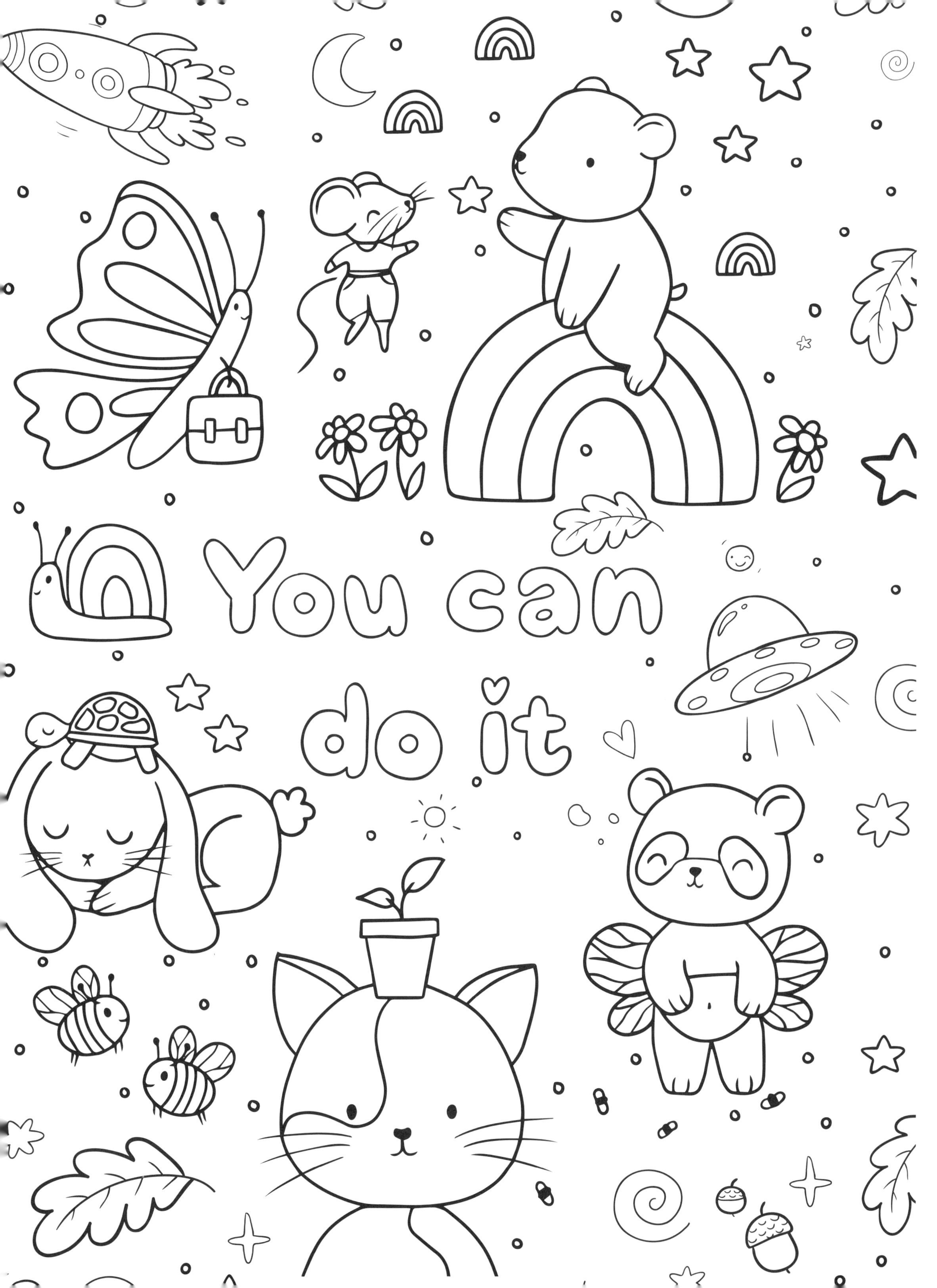
You can
do it

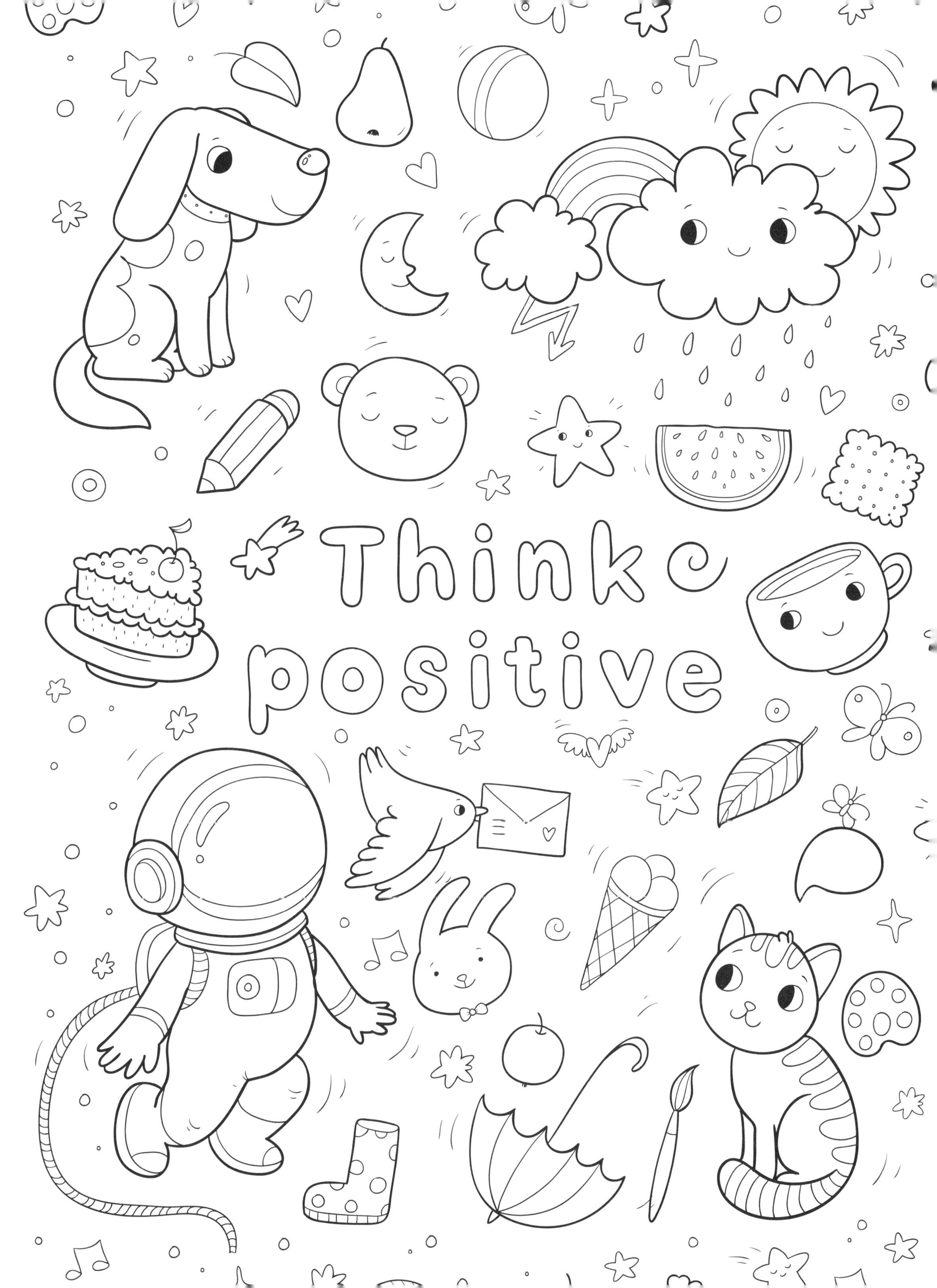
Think
positive